The Smart Consumer

A Legal Guide to Your Rights in the Marketplace

Author: Wesley J. Smith
Project Director: Theresa Meehan Rudy
Editor: Kay Ostberg
Graphics and Production: David Bell

Our thanks to the following consumer specialists, organizations and attorneys for their invaluable comments and advice: Judy McCoid, Helen Ewing Nelson, Caleen Norrod, People's Medical Society and Katherine Wertheim.

ISBN 0-910073-20-1

Also by HALT:
Using a Lawyer
Probate
Real Estate
Small Claims Court
Everyday Contracts
Using the Law Library
If You Want to Sue a Lawyer
    ... A Directory of Legal Malpractice Attorneys
Legal Rights for Seniors
You, Your Family and the Law
Your Guide to Living Trusts and Other Trusts

TABLE OF CONTENTS

PART 4   CREDIT & DEALING WITH DEBT

APPENDICES

INTRODUCTION

Each and every one of us are consumers. Virtually every day we purchase goods and services, be it grocery shopping, buying a car, calling a plumber, going to the doctor or the myriad of other large and small business transactions we are involved in as we go about the daily tasks of living.

Until the last few decades, this was a daunting situation. The Latin term *caveat emptor* (buyer beware) symbolized the fact that consumers were, for the most part, on their own. The government did little, if anything, to regulate the marketplace, and consumers often had a difficult time enforcing the few legal rights they did have against those who sold shoddy goods and services.

Today, thanks to a century of citizen activism, the situation has changed. There is now a vast and intricate system in place specifically designed to protect you in the marketplace. More than ever before, you have the power to enforce fairness, truth and safety in the marketplace. This book is intended to inform you about these systems and what you can do to enhance your power and consumer effectiveness.

A WORD ABOUT TERMS

You don't need a law degree to use this book. Yet, a discussion of your legal rights in the marketplace invariably turns up legal words and phrases that may be foreign to you at first. Some quick examples include lemon laws, breach, deposition and warranty. Every time a new legal term or phrase is used in this book, it is printed in italics. A glossary (Appendix 5) has been included at the end of the book to assist you.

HOW TO USE THIS BOOK

Designed as a reference text, this book can be read from cover to cover, but its most important use will be as a resource during a time of need. In fact, within these pages, you should be able to find a discussion of the most common legal problems that relate to the issues facing consumers.

The book is divided into four separate sections. The first deals with the various systems that exist to protect your rights. There you will find a complete discussion of how the legal system works, what your administrative remedies are, and when to turn to alternative dispute resolution programs. The second part of this book covers your rights when purchasing products, especially automobiles and houses. The third part deals with issues you need to know about obtaining services, in particular, getting your auto repaired and, dealing with attorneys, physicians, insurance agents and building contractors. Finally, in this credit-happy economy, we will touch on the issues you need to know about obtaining credit and dealing with debt.

DEALING WITH PROFESSIONALS

Although this book gives a general description of the law, it cannot give you legal advice based on your individual circumstances. However, most of the time, the information you receive in these pages should be sufficient for you to understand your rights and conduct your affairs from a position of knowledge and insight. Areas where you may want to consult a professional are flagged. You may also want to explore other books that give more detail about a particular subject. Additional resources are listed in the bibliography.

PART 1

KNOWLEDGE
IS POWER

1

CONSUMER RIGHTS
& THE LAW

In recent decades, a revolution has occurred in this country that has created a system that has added significantly to the power of consumers. The key to taking advantage of your rights is your desire to take advantage of the opportunities this system presents. To do that, you have to understand how the "system," designed to protect you, operates. This chapter will serve as an introduction to this system, including the topics of federal regulation, state regulation, and an overview of private legal remedies available to you to enforce your legal rights.

Since most consumer controversies involve contract law, it helps to know something about how contracts are formed. Our discussion begins here.

CONTRACT LAW

It is often said that the basic right to make a deal, even a bad one, is found in the U.S. Constitution. In fact, the underlying principle of the marketplace is that once a bargain is made, it should be upheld. This promotes predictability and protects everyone's right to make a deal.

A contract is any agreement between two or more people that is enforceable in court. It involves a "meeting of the minds" among the contracting parties to do or not do something in exchange for something else. A valid contract exists if you have:

- **An offer, counteroffer and acceptance.** (One side makes an offer and the other side accepts it or makes a counteroffer. If a counteroffer is made, a valid contract does not exist until the counteroffer is accepted.)
- **Consideration.** (This occurs when each side provides the other with some benefit. For example one side supplies a product or service, the other pays for it.)
- **Itemized terms.** (These are the details that define what the rights and responsibilities are of each side in the contract. For example, who is making the contract and what the property or service, time, place, price and other details are.)
- **No valid defenses.** (A contract doesn't exist if it was entered into for illegal purposes or if there is some other valid defense.)

Most contracts can be oral or in writing to be enforceable. (There are some contracts that must be in writing; for example, purchases of real property.)

If one party to a contract breaks the promise and does not perform, it is called a *breach of contract.* There are several remedies—in- or out-of-court— that may be available to you if your contract has been breached. Out-of-court remedies are discussed in Chapter 3. In court, you can request:

1) *Money Damages:* The usual remedy available for breach of contract is a court judgment awarding the injured party money damages. How much money? An amount sufficient to compensate for the loss caused by the breach of contract, the idea being to place the injured party in the same position as he or she would be in had the contract been fully performed.

> Peter contracted with Alice to paint his house. They agreed that he would pay her $2,000 and that he would buy the paint and pay $500 down. Alice was to have the job completed by June 1. Alice started the job but never completed it. Peter then hired Debra to complete the job. Debra charged $2,200 to complete the job, which Peter paid. Peter sued Alice in

small claims court and received a judgment for $700—the difference between the $2,700 Peter paid for the paint job ($500 to Alice plus $2,200 to Debra) and the $2,000 original contract price.

2) *Specific Performance:* In most contract cases performance cannot be compelled by a court. Thus, in the example above, Alice could not be forced to complete the paint job but could be compelled to pay money damages. However, there are some cases where the subject matter is considered so unique that performance will be compelled.

> Mary agreed to buy Mike's house. After the contract was signed Mike changed his mind and agreed to pay Mary reasonable money damages. Mary didn't want money. She wanted the house. The court's awarded Mary specific performance and forced Mike to sell the house because all real property is considered unique. The real estate sales contract also called for Mary to buy Mike's refrigerator. Mike refused to leave it with the house. Mary asked the court to order specific performance. The court refused because the refrigerator was not original or unique. However, Mary was awarded $500, which represented the fair market value of the refrigerator.

3) *Injunctions:* An injunction can compel or prevent action. In a very few cases, a court will issue an injunction when a contract has been breached. For example, if you have purchased a house and then the seller tries to convey the property to someone else, you can obtain an injunction to prevent the change in title.

Other Reasons For Suing

You Can Sue If a Tort was Committed. A *tort* is a civil wrong (other than a breach of contract). A tort can be based on unintentional conduct, i.e., negligence or on intentional misconduct.

If you have been the victim of a tort, you can sue for money to compensate you for your damages. Thus, if you buy a defective product and you are injured by it, you can sue for your damages. If you have been the victim of intentional misrepresentation, you can sue for the tort of fraud.

In tort law, there are different ways that damages are measured:

1) *Compensatory Damages:* These are out-of-pocket losses. For example, if a product was purchased based on misrepresentation, the cost of the product purchased because of the fraud is the out-of-pocket expense. Or, if an injury resulted from the use of an unsafe product, the cost of medical care and lost wages are out-of-pocket damages which may be compensated.

2) *Pain and Suffering:* In an injury case you can receive money to compensate you for pain and suffering you have experienced and/or will experience, sometimes including emotional suffering. This is not a remedy that is available in contract law.

3) *Punitive Damages:* In rare cases, if the tort was intentional or especially outrageous, damages may be collected above and beyond compensatory damages or pain and suffering. This is known as punitive damages because the intent behind the award is to punish the wrongdoer and deter others from engaging in malicious or outrageous misconduct.

Many laws regulate our contracts. These range from "common law" principles, derived by our courts from early English precedents, to state laws that govern the buying and selling of goods and services, most of them variations on what's known as the Uniform Commercial Code. Several federal agencies, like those mentioned in the next section, also enforce laws that regulate contracts and protect consumers.

GOVERNMENT REGULATION

The consumer movement first achieved sustained success during the heyday of the Progressive Movement between 1900 and the end of World War I. During these years the governing economic philosophy changed. Rather than permit a *laissez faire* philosophy to dominate (the idea that business should be left alone by government), the belief took hold that one way that government could promote the public good was to curb business excesses through a rational system of regulation. Important reforms were implemented. For example, the Federal Trade Commission (FTC) was established to prevent the use of unfair and deceptive advertising practices. Government meat inspections increased and the conservation movement was born, the precursor of today's environmental movement.

During the Great Depression of the 1930s, the regulatory role of government increased further. The Federal Communications Commission (FCC) was created to govern the use of broadcast airways. The Securities and Exchange Commission (SEC) began its important oversight work over stock exchanges and issues of business investment. The Federal Drug Administration (FDA) was created to oversee the research and marketing of medicinal drugs.

The next leap forward came during the 1960s and 1970s. Personified by attorney Ralph Nader, a new consumer movement was created which energetically pushed for increased government and private actions to protect consumers. As a result, new auto safety standards were created, truth-in-lending laws were enacted, and various consumer protection statutes were put in place at the federal, state and local levels. At last, buyers of goods and services had real clout in government and in the marketplace. As a result, accountability exists in the system. Cars, among many other products, are now safer, food is generally more pure and people are less likely to take misleading or fraudulent behavior sitting down.

The Role of Government Regulation

Federal, state and local governments provide many forms of consumer protection. This is done in a variety of ways, each of which fills an important consumer protection niche:

Writing the Rules. A major function of government regulation, whether federal, state or local, is the promulgation of rules and laws that govern how business may operate. These laws range from those specifically aimed at protecting consumer safety such as airline safety regulations, to economic matters, such as rate regulation of utilities.

Enforcing Rules. All of the rules in the world wouldn't do much good unless they could be enforced. Thus, in addition to writing laws and regulations, a major function of many government regulatory agencies is enforcement. For example, the FTC will investigate deceptive business practices and exact punishment if abuse is found to occur. Likewise, state licensing agencies will investigate complaints against licensed professionals such as doctors or building contractors and discipline those found to have acted unethically. Such discipline often includes paying consumers for damages incurred. Sometimes, the regulatory agencies will also refer cases to criminal enforcement authorities, thereby allowing law enforcement greater latitude and scope. (However, keep in mind that such enforcement can be slow or limited by budget problems. Thus, you may have to act as the "squeaky wheel.")

Educating the Public. Another important function of governmental agencies is to inform the public of their rights and responsibilities and to assist consumers in making wise buying choices. Thus, the U.S. Department of Agriculture supplies nutritional publications to consumers and state insurance commissions offer comparisons of insurance company consumer complaint ratios.

How the Government Can Help

The government helps consumers by:

Preventing Problems. Government regulation acts as a deterrent to much misconduct. Business operators know that they must act within defined parameters or risk government sanction. This in and of itself prevents a great deal of abuse. After all, no one likes to fight city hall. Also, through their public information activities, agencies arm consumers with important information that helps them protect themselves from shoddy business practices and illegal or unethical activities. (Unfortunately, not all shoddy and unethical business practices are prevented. Thus, your personal consumer protection radar should always be alert to trouble.)

Assisting Consumers With Grievances. Consumers who complain to local agencies and regulatory agencies often find that their grievances are redressed by the agency through a process known as *administrative action.* On occasion, especially after repeated violations, such action will be a lawsuit brought by the government on behalf of the complaining citizen, thereby relieving the citizen from having to take such action in their own name and on their own dime. At other times, the government will offer mediation services to help buyers and sellers resolve their differences. If many consumers have complained, direct administrative punishment, such as fines or loss of a professional license, may be imposed. (Since the agency may be reluctant to act absent a high level of abuse, your complaint is important, since it can add to a chorus of voices pushing for government intervention.)

There can be no doubt that government regulation and enforcement offer a powerful and often underutilized tool in enforcing consumer rights. Details about the work of various government agencies and how they can specifically assist you will be described throughout the book as they are relevant to specific topics.

THE CIVIL JUSTICE SYSTEM

Buyers of goods and services also need to know about their rights under the civil justice system. The civil justice system permits individuals to enforce their legal rights, usually, but not always, in a court of law. The balance of this chapter will introduce you to this system. You should realize, however, that the vast majority of consumer disputes can be and are settled out-of-court. The ways in which these disputes are typically handled are covered in Chapter 3, Enforcing Your Rights.

Understanding the Court System

The courts in the United States can be divided into the following categories: local courts, state courts and federal courts.

Local Courts. Smaller cases are heard in local courts, often called municipal court or justice court. Smaller courts are usually made up of a general trial court and small claims court.

If you have a landlord/tenant dispute, are involved in a minor accident or have a contract dispute involving a relatively small amount of money, it will probably be heard in a local trial court. Small claims courts are reserved for matters involving small amounts of money (the maximum amount that can be in dispute will vary from jurisdiction to jurisdiction) where the case will be heard quickly and inexpensively and best of all, usually without lawyers. However, corporations involved in small claims court cases can be represented by a lawyer. Appeals from local court decisions are usually heard in state superior courts. (Procedures where you live may differ.) For more information on small claims court, see Chapter 3.

State Courts. State courts resolve civil disputes of all kinds and nature, ranging from breach of contract and fraud to divorce and business disputes. Consumers' disputes, especially over "big ticket" items, such as real property purchases and medical and legal malpractice cases, usually are heard in state courts.

State courts are also generally made up of three levels; trial courts (usually called Superior Court), appellate courts (sometimes called the Court of Appeals), and the highest court (often called the Supreme Court).

The state courts of appeal and state supreme courts work in ways similar to the federal system. The United States Supreme Court can be turned to after state courts have ruled, if, and only if, the question raised involves federal issues.

The Federal Courts. Most disputes cannot be litigated in federal court. That is because the *jurisdiction* (power to act) of the federal courts is restricted by law. Generally, federal courts handle criminal and civil cases involving the alleged violation of federal law or the claimed deprivation of rights guaranteed by federal statute or the United States Constitution. For example, bankruptcy cases (see Chapter 14) are all handled in Federal Bankruptcy Courts. There are also restricted occasions when a legal dispute involving state law will end up in federal court. Usually, this occurs when citizens of two different states are involved in litigation involving large sums of money (known as "diversity of citizenship" jurisdiction).

Federal courts are generally divided into three levels: trial courts (Federal District Courts, Bankruptcy Courts, etc.), the Circuit Court of Appeals (there are 9 Circuits in the United States) and the United States Supreme Court. The Court of Appeals will review any trial court decision upon proper request, although few cases are appealed. Most appeals are not successful. There is no legal right to have a matter heard before the United States Supreme Court (with a very few exceptions not relevant here), and the court will only take for consideration those cases which it deems to be of special national importance or to resolve differences in law application among the circuits. It is the rare case indeed that meets tough Supreme Court criteria.

Administrative Law Courts. If you seek assistance from a government regulatory agency, be it state or federal, and the agency decides to take your case, it will probably be heard in an administrative law proceeding. These hearings tend to be less formal and have less restrictive rules of evidence.

It has been said that the law is a great equalizer. This is true—if people know their rights, have the time and understand how to enforce them. This chapter has served as an introduction to the legal system and some of the basic laws that exist to protect you and help you enforce your rights. Details on how the system actually works (what you need to do to file a lawsuit in court) will be supplied in Chapter 3. But first, let's discuss some of the things you can do in the conduct of your personal business that will help you exercise power and clout in the marketplace and which can help you use the legal system effectively should you ever have to resort to administrative or legal remedies.

2

HOPE FOR THE BEST, PREPARE FOR THE WORST

Exercising power in the marketplace does not happen by accident. Like a body builder increasing his or her muscle mass through exercise, you have to increase your consumer strength by taking a thoughtful and organized approach to your buying. In essence, you have to become a professional consumer. This is a two-tiered approach:

First: Avoiding trouble in the first place by making informed and rational buying choices.

Second: Having the resources and evidence at your disposal to win if, despite your best efforts at exercising consumer excellence, you have to fight for your rights.

BEFORE YOU BUY

Effective buying begins long before the purchase is actually made. Buyer dissatisfaction often occurs because of miscommunication. On occasion, unscrupulous sellers simply misrepresent their products or services. More often, miscommunication happens because buyers are not sufficiently informed about what they are buying and sellers don't adequately inform their customers. This can lead to buying decisions based on things such as:

- "Wishful thinking" assuming facts about the product or service provider that are not true
- The emotion of the moment (sometimes known as impulse buying)
- Succumbing to high-pressure sales tactics
- Some other reason for purchasing not based solely on the purchaser's true wants and desires

Buying based on any of the above often leads to disappointment. The best way to avoid these hazards and make sure you are buying what you really want is to prepare ahead of time. This takes some research. Let's say you want to buy a new stereo. Write down a list of the things you need to know. For example, you might want to learn:

- What features are usually available in the price range I want to pay?
- What "options" do I want and which can I live without?
- What are the warranties for stereos?
- Who will do the repair service if there is a problem?
- What is the return policy of each store I shop at?
- What are the brands in the marketplace and how do they compare to each other for sound quality and durability?
- etc.

Once you figure out what you need to know in order to make an informed decision, you should go about obtaining the necessary knowledge. There are many ways to obtain it. One excellent source is *Consumer Reports* magazine, which compares products and services and rates the quality of the products and services surveyed based on a wide range of criteria. *Consumer Reports* magazine is an especially good resource, because of their reputation for integrity and product knowledge and the fact that they take no advertising and conduct their own tests. Back issues of the magazine can be found in your library. Other sources of information are from product manufacturers, industry group consumer information services, comparative shopping, and by reading the many books published each year on various consumer concerns. Also, friends are a good source of information about products and services based on their real-life experiences or special expertise they may possess.

Once you think you know enough to make an intelligent buying decision, the time has come to comparison shop. Now is the time to exercise consumer power by basing your decision on rational considerations rather than high-pressure sales or the emotion of the moment. (There is a societal benefit to all of this. The more consumers buy based on an intelligent approach, the better the marketplace will be because slick and shoddy operators will not be able to compete in the marketplace.)

When shopping, it is a good idea to write down the information you obtain. This will come in handy when making your buying decision. It will also help you recall the information you were given which you may need if you run into trouble.

Once you buy, be sure and keep the notes you took during your shopping in your personal records. Also, keep the card of the salesperson who sold you the product. In that way, if you are satisfied, you can refer the person business. On the other hand, if there is a problem, that is where you will want to go first for satisfaction.

Get it In Writing

Always try to get promises and representations from sales personnel, manufacturers or service providers in writing. This can be in the form of a brochure, a letter of representation, or handwritten notes on a business card. For example, assume that you have decided to purchase a dog based on an advertisement in the newspaper. In your research on the topic of buying pets, you have read that disease can sometimes be a problem in pet purchases. You have visited the dog owner and fallen in love with the dog but have told the owner you are hesitating because you are afraid of the expense if the dog gets sick. In response, the owner promises to pay you for any out-of-pocket expenses incurred if the dog gets sick within six months and to return your money if the dog dies within the first three months. Have the owner write down the promise and any other representations that might have been made as part of the receipt of sale. In that way, if there is a problem and you have to enforce your rights in small claims court or some other venue (see Chapter 3), you can avoid the problem of "It's my word against yours."

AFTER YOU BUY

Your work as a professional buyer does not end once the purchase has been made.

Maintain Your Records

You should organize your personal business transactions just as you would if you were conducting a commercial enterprise. This isn't complicated. Any stationery store will sell you file folders that can be used for this purpose, which can then be broken down into different topics, such as electronic product purchases, lawyer, doctor, etc. Keep written items in your file such as receipts, sales brochures, instruction books, warranties, and correspondence. Then, if you have questions you will know where to find answers in a quick and efficient way. That can save a lot of time and bother. Moreover, your records can prove invaluable in effectively presenting your side of the story, should you have to seek redress from the seller.

Now, there is no doubt that taking this time and effort to keep accurate records can be a nuisance. But there is a big payoff: power in the marketplace. We will discuss how this power can serve you, below and in Chapter 3.

Learn the Art of Effective Complaining

The last thing you want to have to do is to take formal action to enforce your rights. Not only can such action be time consuming and emotionally upsetting, but, depending on the circumstances, it can be quite expensive. Your better approach is to try and solve your problem informally, directly, with the seller through *complaining*. Happily, most problems that consumers face can be resolved in this manner.

Complaining should be approached in an organized and businesslike way. Here are some tips:

Start Off Assuming the Seller's Goodwill. One of the big mistakes people make when they first complain is to assume that the seller is their adversary. Often, this simply isn't true. (Besides, as the old saying goes, you can catch more flies with honey than with vinegar.) Remember, sellers, whether of products or services, have a vested interest in your satisfaction. They want your repeat business and they want you to refer your friends and loved ones to them. Thus, assume that the seller will want to help solve your problem, not that they will resist your call for justice.

Be Courteous. No one likes to be treated in a demeaning or adversarial way. This is simply a matter of human nature. If you begin complaining in an angry and accusative fashion, you are much more likely to be met with defensive resistance than if you treat the seller with respect.

Be Assertive. Being courteous is not the same thing as being a milk toast. Rather, the person who is courteous is deemed as coming from a place of strength. And, when courtesy is mixed with quiet assertiveness, the result is an aura of confidence that tells the seller, "I know my rights. I know how to assert myself. Now, let's work together to fashion a solution to my problem."

Avoid Emotionalism. A complaint is a business transaction, not a family argument. Emotionalism is unlikely to win friends or influence people. And, while being liked is not your objective, it helps. Besides, imagine how you would react if faced with an enraged or distraught complainer.

Be Specific. This is where your record keeping comes in. The more specific you can be in demonstrating the righteousness of your complaint, the more likely you are to achieve satisfaction. For example, assume you have purchased a vacuum cleaner and are unhappy with its performance.

The Wrong Approach

Hey! This vacuum I bought is a piece of junk! I don't know when I bought it but I know it was only a short time ago. Give me my money back!

The Right Approach

Two weeks ago, I purchased this vacuum cleaner. Here is the receipt. Your sales brochure which I have brought with me specifically states that the vacuum will pick up cat hair. It takes several passes with the machine to pick up my cat's hair and even then, I have to use a brush to get all of the hair off my couch. I would like my money back.

Be Willing to Be Wrong. Everyone makes mistakes. This includes complaining consumers. Perhaps the consumer believes a machine is not working when he or she simply does not know how to operate it properly. Or, maybe the consumer has unreasonable expectations and expects to receive more than the product can deliver. Thus, when you complain, you should be sure to listen carefully. Not only is this respectful but you may find that there is really no problem at all. Besides, if you are wrong, all of the complaining and legal action in the world is not going to make you right.

Ask to Speak to a Supervisor. If you don't receive satisfaction at the entry level of complaining, ask to speak to a supervisor. (A salesperson may not have authority to do what you have asked.) You may be angry at this point but be sure to continue to remain calm and to present your argument in a calm and businesslike fashion. Often, a supervisor will give knowledgeable and courteously-assertive customers the benefit of the doubt rather than risk losing their goodwill and future business.

Go to the Top

If your initial complaints don't achieve your desired results, go to the top. Courteously, get the name and address of the manager, regional supervisor or CEO of the company and let the salesperson or supervisor know you intend to pursue the matter at that level. If that doesn't resolve the matter, follow through.

At this point, everything should be handled in a more formal manner since you will be preparing for formal enforcement actions if going to the top does not produce an acceptable accommodation.

Put Everything in Writing. There may be a natural tendency of upper management to back up their people. Thus, you will want to present your argument as thoroughly as you can. This is done most effectively by letter. Here is a sample complaint letter:

QuickClean Vacuum Company
Attn: Joan Parker, CEO
(Address)

Dear Ms. Parker:

On September 3, 1994, I purchased your Model A-100 vacuum cleaner. I have enclosed a copy of the receipt. Your salesperson, John Gage, promised me that the machine would pick up cat hair on my couch without my having to purchase any additional attachments. That was an important factor in my purchasing decision. Your brochure (copy enclosed) also indicates that the vacuum is excellent at picking up cat hair. I am sorry to report that I am dissatisfied with the vacuum I purchased. Simply stated, it does not pick up cat hair.

On September 18, 1994, I brought this to the attention of Mr. Gage. He told me that I would have to buy a special attachment to pick up the cat hair. When I reminded him of his representation to me, he denied that was what he said. (I am enclosing a copy of the notes I took during Mr. Gage's sales presentation. Note that I have underlined the statement, "Will pick up cat hair.") When I spoke to Mr. Gage's supervisor, she too told me that I would have to buy an attachment and refused to give me my money back.

I intend to pursue this matter in Small Claims Court if necessary and to complain to the Better Business Bureau and the Department of Consumer Affairs. However, I want to give you the opportunity of handling this matter without further action. During the day, I can be reached at 555-2222. My evening number is 555-3333. My address is on this letterhead.

If I have not heard from you within two weeks of the date of this letter, I will assume that you do not intend to return my money and I shall act accordingly.

Very truly yours,

A good letter of complaint is specific as to time and place, tells the reader what happened in a concise and understandable fashion, names the dates and people involved, asks for a specific remedy and sets a reasonable time by which such action should occur. Your letter should only address the complaint at hand. Don't use your letter to complain about non-related issues, such as the store's hours of operation.

Now assume that you receive a call in response to your letter of complaint and you are offered the necessary attachments at manufacturer's cost. You decide to take the deal as a compromise. You should send a confirming letter, setting forth in concrete terms the agreement that has been reached. Here is an example:

Dear Ms. Parker:

> Thank you for your kind telephone call of December 2. I wish to confirm the agreement we reached at that time. You offered to sell me for $10 (the manufacturer's cost) the attachment model D-34 for use with my vacuum in cleaning cat hair. I have accepted this compromise on condition that I receive the attachment within 10 days. You have advised me that I should contact the store salesman, Mr. Gage, to make the arrangements for pick up. If this is not to your understanding, please contact me at your earliest convenience.
> Thank you for restoring my faith in your company.

Very truly yours,

A confirming letter should be used frequently in most of your business transactions because they preserve an accurate record of your business dealings should you ever need to recall what was said and by whom in the past. Confirming letters can also serve as evidence in the event that a dispute ends up in court or *alternative dispute resolution* (ADR).

Complain to Those Who Can Help

If, despite all of your reasonable efforts to work things out, you are unable to obtain satisfaction, you will have a choice to make: either you will drop the matter or seek to formally enforce your rights (see Chapter 3). However, before taking either path, there is one more thing you can do that may help you: Call in consumer reinforcements from the outside. Here are a few ideas:

Media Programs. Many television, newspaper and radio stations provide a consumer "hot line" or "action" service. If your problem would make an interesting story (and even if it wouldn't) contact your local media to see if it has a consumer reporter that will go to bat for you. Often, the prospect of media publicity will overcome intransigence and allow a reasonable solution. You can find out if your community has a media-sponsored program by simply calling your local newspaper and radio and television stations, and asking if they have a consumer reporter.

Complain to the Better Business Bureau. The Better Business Bureau in your area may have a mediation or arbitration service or may be otherwise able to intervene to help resolve the matter. (Some Bureau chapters are more effective than others.) Thus, if you find that you can't resolve the matter on an individual basis, contact your nearest BBB and ask for their assistance. (Their address and telephone number will be in your local telephone book.)

Complain to the Local or State Department of Consumer Affairs. Most localities have a consumer affairs office to help people who have been taken advantage of. If you believe that you have been treated in a way that may be against the law, try calling the state. (Send a copy of your letter of complaint to the offending business. That alone may be enough to get them to soften their position.)

After receiving your letter, you will be contacted by a worker from the agency. You may be asked to fill out a complaint form or otherwise provide further information. Be sure to act promptly and completely on all requests. The more seriously you take your problem, the more likely the agency will too.

Complain to a Trade Association. Some businesses have trade associations that can put pressure on a member who is not adequately serving the public or which will serve as a go-between when a member has a dispute with a customer or client. If your dispute involves a business which is affiliated with the association, contact the group to see if they can help. If the business that you are having a dispute with brags about their membership in the organization, this can be an especially effective strategy.

Complain to a Licensing Board. If the business you have a complaint against is licensed by the state (e.g., lawyers, doctors, building contractors, etc.) their misbehavior may subject them to official discipline. Don't be too enthusiastic about your chances of recovery, though. The attorney discipline system, for example, is riddled with flaws: More than 90,000 complaints are filed each year with these agencies, but only about two percent of the complaints result in more than private reprimand, and these agencies don't provide any compensation. Similar problems exist with other licensing boards. Nevertheless, consumers who have problems with lawyers, doctors, contractors and the like, should file complaints with these agencies if only to document those problems. It might be sufficient to get justice and may also serve as a protector of the rest of society against an unethical practitioner, especially if the problem is of a severe nature and numerous complaints have been filed already.

If you complain to outside sources, you may be asked to fill out a complaint form or otherwise document your side of the story. This is another place where your record keeping can be put to good use. Having all of the important documents of your transaction at hand will allow you to tell your story in an organized and methodical fashion and support your allegations with specific documentary proof. This can be important since the righteousness of your gripe will be at least partially judged on the quality of your presentation.

For more information, write for a free copy of *Consumer's Resource Handbook,* Consumer Information Center, Pueblo, CO 81009. This handbook provides addresses and telephone numbers of businesses, state and local consumer protection offices and federal government agencies.

Now, let's turn to a closer look at the various methods by which you can enforce your rights, ranging from going to court to using ADR to seeking the assistance of specific government agencies.

3

ENFORCING
YOUR RIGHTS

Knowing your rights is one thing. Getting out there and enforcing them is sometimes quite another. That's because pursuing your rights, especially when forced to do so in court, can be a time-consuming, complicated and expensive endeavor. (Often, unnecessarily complicated and expensive.) This sometimes makes people reluctant to forge ahead.

SMALL CLAIMS COURT

The easiest court procedure to understand is that of small claims court. The vast majority of states have small claims courts. States that don't will hear disputes involving small amounts of money (say under $2,500) in their lowest court (i.e., municipal or justice court). While the rules governing small claims courts differ from state-to-state, the basics are similar.

If you are going to seek redress for a consumer complaint, small claims court is usually an excellent place to go. This is true for several reasons:

• **It's Easy:** While there are rules that must be followed in small claims court (see below), they are easy to understand and apply.

- **It's Inexpensive:** Small claims court is designed to give you access to justice without incurring the costs and lawyers' fees that are often necessary if you become involved with other court proceedings.
- **It May Exclude Lawyers:** In some states, lawyers are not permitted in small claims court. Even in those that do permit attorneys, litigants often do not retain a lawyer because of the cost of paying the lawyer versus the amount of money at stake. The absence of lawyer participation saves a lot of time and complication. Corporations often are represented by lawyers, but they must comply with the same simplified small claims court procedures that you do and thus do not have an unfair advantage.
- **It's Fast:** One of the major problems with the civil justice system today is the fact that it often takes years to obtain justice. Thankfully, this is not true in small claims court. Once a case is filed in court, it is usually only a matter of several weeks before the matter is before a judge.
- **It's Effective:** A *judgment* in small claims court is as good as a judgment in any other court and can be enforced in the same manner. And a judgment can be renewed periodically if the person you are trying to collect from skips town or otherwise makes the judgment difficult to collect.

How to Proceed

If you believe you have a grievance which should be brought to small claims court, here are the steps you should take (procedures in your area may vary):

Step 1: Try and Resolve the Matter Informally. The best court experience is not having to go to court at all. This can sometimes be accomplished by writing a letter to the person or business you believe has wronged you and (politely) demanding redress. Here's an example of a demand letter:

November 13, 1994
Inept Dry Cleaners
Attn: John Clumsy, Owner
4444 Notwithit Lane
Cedar City, NM 00000
RE: Damages to my suit after dry cleaning

Dear Mr. Clumsy:

As you may recall, on November 4, 1993, I brought my blue suede suit to your cleaning establishment for professional cleaning. (Copy of receipt enclosed.) On November 7, I picked the suit up and noticed that the color had badly faded and that there were many spots on the fabric, which looked as if bleach had been spilled upon it. The suit has been ruined.

You offered to give me $100 for damages, an amount you claimed would be sufficient to redye the fabric. But that is not sufficient. I bought the suit new only 3 months ago for $950. (Copy of receipt enclosed.) I believe that I am entitled to the full amount because the suit was new and the problems with the suit are not those that should have been associated with usual cleaning methods.

Please forward the $950 to me on or before November 25. Should you not do so, I shall have no choice but to pursue the matter in a court of law. I can be reached during the day at 555-5555. My home phone number is 555-1111. My address is on this letterhead. Thank you for your cooperation.

Very truly yours,

The demand letter should be polite, businesslike and to the point. Avoid emotionalism or name calling. After all, you want to solve a problem, not start a fight. It should also set a reasonable time for compliance so that you can proceed to the next step if you do not receive satisfaction.

Step 2: Figure Out What Your Case Is Worth. Small claims courts put a cap on the amount of money you can obtain, typically between $1,500 and $5,000, depending on the locale. This is known as the "jurisdictional limit" of the court. For example, assume the small claims court in your area has a jurisdictional limit of $2,500. (The jurisdictional limit of small claims court will vary from state-to-state.) No matter how much your case is worth, the damages that could be awarded to you would be limited to $2,500, or less. (That does not mean that you cannot file your $3,000 case in small claims court. You just could not obtain the full amount you were owed.)

If your case comes within or close to the jurisdictional limit, move on to Step 3. If your case is worth much more, and you're not willing to settle for the small claims court limit, skip to the next section. (Bringing a Lawsuit.)

You also need to know the basis for your suit. Thus, if a contract was broken, you need to be able to prove the existence of the contract. If you were the victim of *negligence,* you need to be able to show the nature of the negligence and how the negligence harmed you. If some other law has been broken, such as a former landlord refusing to return a security deposit, you need to know your rights under that law. To find out more about the possible basis for your claim you might take a trip to your local law library. (Most court houses have a law library available to the public, as do many law schools.)

Step 3: File the Complaint. Small claims court is initiated by filing a *complaint.* The complaint is a simple form that you obtain from the small claims court clerk. The form will explain how to prepare the complaint. Once you have filled it out, hand it to the clerk and pay the filing fee. Filing fees are usually less than $10. The clerk will set a trial date and you will receive a copy of the complaint back and a *summons* form, a document that tells the person you are suing that he or she is being brought to court.

Step 4: Serve the Complaint and Summons on the Defendant. Under our system, the *defendant* (the person being sued), has a right to notice of the hearing and to be advised of the nature of the complaint against them. This is done by having a copy of the summons and complaint served on the defendant. This can be done by a professional process server, the marshal or sheriff. (There will be a charge for this service. Keep a record of this expense because if you win the case the defendant can be made to reimburse you.) You can also have a friend serve the document if they are not involved in the case. If you go this route, be sure they fill out a proof-of-service form, which can be obtained from the court clerk. If a sheriff or process server serves process, you will receive the proof-of-service form from them in the mail. (Some jurisdictions permit you to serve the summons and complaint by registered or certified mail. Ask the court clerk about the best method of service in your area. However, most jurisdictions do not allow *you* to serve the person you are serving.)

Once the defendant is served, he or she will have the right to file a response. This is usually called the *answer.* Answers usually deny the claim. If the defendant believes he or she has a cause against you, they can file a *counterclaim* seeking money from you. The answer (and counterclaim) will be mailed to you. If you are sued, you must also file an answer. The form is available from the court clerk or it will be mailed to you with the counterclaim.

Step 5: Prepare Your Case. This is your chance to play Clarence Darrow, and you want to make sure you are prepared. Thus, gather together all of the documents you intend to show the judge, round up your witnesses (if any) and make sure they are going to be able to go to court with you. If you need to do some legal research, go to the law library. Prepare your case in an orderly fashion. Remember, your job will be to persuade the judge that you are right. This is best done by presenting the case in an orderly, logical manner that will allow him or her to understand your grievance. (You will only have a short time to present your case so being prepared is the key.)

Step 6: Go to Court. Be sure to arrive on time. (You may be asked to check in with the court clerk. If in doubt, ask.) If you are not there on time and your case is called, the judge may likely dismiss your claim and you will have to start all over again. Also, be sure all of your witnesses are there. (If a witness is unwilling to voluntarily appear for you he or she will have to be *subpoenaed.* The court clerk will have the forms.) You should also dress appropriately. Small claims court is a less formal proceeding than other trial settings but it is still a court of law. Respect for the judge and the court is important, especially since you want to be well thought of. (Men should wear a coat and tie; women should dress in appropriate business clothes.)

The conduct of a trial in small claims court is usually informal. If you are suing, you go first when the judge asks you to present your case. When you make your presentation, lay out the facts in an orderly manner and support it with documents whenever you can. Tell the judge about any witnesses you have and have them ready to tell their story. Be polite, call the judge "your Honor" and otherwise conduct your case in a concise and businesslike manner. (Practicing in front of a mirror before you go to court will help you.) When the other side is presenting their points, *do not interrupt.* Take notes on how you want to reply and hold your fire until the judge tells you it is your turn. Also, be sure to mention that you request reimbursement for the costs of bringing suit (filing fee, service of process fee, etc.).

Once the judge has heard enough, he or she will issue a ruling. A written judgment will be issued by the clerk. Sometimes, the judge takes the matter "under submission." This means you will receive the court's ruling by mail.

Step 7: Be Prepared for an Appeal. After court, there may be an appeal by the defendant, if he or she has lost the case. (Plaintiffs who lose their case are usually not permitted to appeal, but that is not true everywhere.) The appeal will be held in the trial court and is, in effect, a retrial. Prepare your case in the same manner as at the small claims court level. *Note:* Lawyers are allowed in small claims court appeals.

Once you have won the case, you have the right to enforce the judgment. First, ask the defendant to pay before leaving the courthouse. (Often, courts will permit defendants to write out a check or to make monthly payments and will help you set up a payment plan.) If the defendant refuses, you can initiate other action such as *garnishing* the defendant's property or wages. (Some people who do not have the time to learn how to pursue their judgment will turn it over to a collection agency. The agency will then collect the judgment for a percentage of the money collected.)

There are more details on preparing and presenting a small claims court case than space permits to be presented here.*

---

* For more information, see *Small Claims Court—Making Your Way Through The System: A Step-by-Step Guide,* by Theresa Meehan Rudy, in association with HALT, Random House, 1990. $8.95.

BRINGING A LAWSUIT

Matters worth more than the small claims court limit are often resolved by filing a lawsuit in "regular" court. Some of the procedures are similar to small claims court and some differ. (Most, but not all, litigants retain a lawyer to assist them.) Here's a map to litigating:

Find Out If You Have A Case

Before resorting to the time-consuming, aggravating and sometimes expensive effort of filing a lawsuit, you should make sure that you have a decent chance of winning. This can be done in several ways:

Research Your Case in the Law Library. There are a lot of books that can help you determine whether you have a case. Some are encyclopedias that give an overview of the law. Other books are statute books that will define various grounds for suit, often called the cause of action. There are also case books that contain judicial decisions that may be useful to you in determining your rights.

The librarian can help you find the books you need. However, legal research is a skill that must be learned.* If you plan to represent yourself, the law library will also have local court rules and other publications that will help you understand the procedures of going to court, including time limits, filing fees, the correct forms for pleadings and other documents, and your responsibilities as a litigant. Be sure you understand these important rules, for if you do not obey them you could have your case thrown out—even if you are right and would be able to prove your case.

Consult a Lawyer. One of the decisions you will have to make is whether to hire a lawyer. However, even if you plan to represent yourself, you may wish to consult with a lawyer to determine whether you have a good case. (Many lawyers offer

---

* See *Using the Law Library, A Nonlawyers' Guide*, HALT, 1988. $6.95.

free or low expense initial consultations.) Law school legal clinics and community-based legal clinics may also offer low cost legal advice—especially for issues such as landlord-tenant disagreements and for disputes with government entities.

Read Books. There are many books on legal subjects that may be germane to your situation. For example, if you bought a new car that has never operated properly, you would want to find books that discuss the legal remedies for new car owners. A publication that describes your state's lemon laws would be particularly helpful.

Decide Whether To Hire a Lawyer. If your consumer problem involves a lot of money or a complicated area of the law, you have to decide whether to retain a lawyer to assist you. Many people, of course, choose to represent themselves. But before making that decision, remember you will be expected by the court to understand and apply both the substantive law and procedure (the way things are done in court) as if you were licensed to practice law. The ins and outs of retaining and working with a lawyer are discussed in Chapter 9.

The Anatomy of a Lawsuit

Lawsuits follow a predictable pattern. Even so, no two lawsuits are alike. Here is an overview of the different stages of a lawsuit:

Pleadings Stage. Lawsuits are initiated through court documents known as *pleadings*. Like small claims court, a lawsuit is started by filing a *complaint*, claim, petition or other court document with the court. (The name of the document will vary depending on the type of case you are bringing.) The complaint must adequately inform the person or entity being sued of the nature of the claim being made. If it does not, the sued party may file a motion with the court to knock you out of court. The defendant must file an answer within the time specified by law (most often 30 days but it may be less depending on the nature of the case) and may, if facts warrant, cross complain against you. If that happens, you too must file an answer within the time allotted by law. Once the initial pleadings are complete, a document is filed to tell the court the case is "at issue." That puts your case in line for a trial date.

Discovery Stage. Movies often like to depict a trial where a surprise witness suddenly appears, changing the whole course of the suit. In real life, that rarely happens. The reason for this is that each party is entitled to know the facts and allegations that the other side is going to rely on in presenting their case. This is accomplished through a process known as *discovery.*

Discovery is accomplished in many ways. Here is a sampling:

Interrogatories: These are written questions that must be answered in writing under oath. The answers must be given to the court within a specified number of days. Because interrogatories have sometimes been used to harass opponents, many courts now limit the number of questions that can be asked or the number of times a party can submit interrogatories. For copies of interrogatory forms, contact the court clerk.

Depositions: This is a transcript of face-to-face questioning under oath in front of a stenographer or tape recorder. The person being questioned can be either the plaintiff, the defendant or a witness who has pertinent information.

Subpoena duces tecum: This legal document orders someone to appear or requires documents to be presented in court. A court clerk can provide you with the necessary form.

Requests for Admissions: This allows you to establish the existence of certain facts by getting the other side to admit that those certain facts are true. If true facts are denied in the response and they are later proved true, there may be a penalty applied against the denying party.

The discovery process is complicated but may get even more complicated than it sounds. First, litigants often do not comply with their discovery responsibilities, and legitimate disputes often arise about the propriety of some of the questions asked or the relevance of the information requested. This frequently happens when litigating against large corporations or insurance companies whose lawyers will make discovery as pleasant as pulling teeth. When that happens, you must file a motion (a request that a judge take specific action) to order the other side to do the right thing. Secondly, if the questions are not asked in the right manner, important information may not be discovered.

Motions: In addition to filing motions to enforce discovery, other court requests can be made while waiting for trial. Most notable is the motion for *summary judgment.* A summary judgment ends the case by finding that one side or the other wins. This is a drastic measure and is only taken if facts giving rise to the request are undisputed, as proven by discovery testimony, witness statements under oath (declarations) and documents, leading to a mandatory legal conclusion based on these facts. Other motions may be for protective orders; for example, to keep information secret, and requests for a court ordered physical examination, if the issue being litigated involves an injury.

Trial Stage. Eventually, the case will be set for trial by the court clerk, who sends a notice of trial date to the parties in the case. (This may come within months or take up to five years, depending on court congestion where the case takes place). At this point several things go on:

Mandatory Settlement Conference: A settlement conference is often a requirement. In the conference, all parties to the case prepare a legal brief for the court stating why they believe their side will prevail. A judge reads the briefs and tries to help the parties settle their case without trial. The majority of lawsuits are settled at this stage (or before the conference by the parties acting on their own). Other cases are referred by the settlement judge to mandatory arbitration. (See below.)

Trial: If the case isn't settled, the matter goes to trial, either before a judge (called a court trial) or a jury. (Not every case goes to a jury. Sometimes the parties don't want one and sometimes, the law does not permit one.) A lot goes into a trial: Pretrial motions about what can be admitted into evidence, trial briefs, subpoenaing witnesses to make sure they appear, etc. After the trial is over, a verdict is entered.

Post Trial: Wait, the fun has only begun. Even if you win, you may feel like a loser. That's because post-trial motions can be filed which seek to change the outcome. For example, a motion for new trial is common as is a request to reduce damages. Sometimes, a request is made for the judge to change the verdict.

Judgment: After all of the wailing and gnashing of teeth by the loser (and sometimes the winner) is expressed through post-trial motions, a judgment will be entered. This is what may be enforced against the losing party.

Appeals. Anyone subject to the judgment can file an appeal. The appellate process can take years, with some cases going all the way up to the U.S. Supreme Court. However, most appeals never get past the initial appellate court and most appeals are unsuccessful.

If the party appealing does not want the judgment to be executed, a bond will usually have to be posted.

ALTERNATIVE DISPUTE RESOLUTION

As this brief discussion of lawsuits clearly shows, trials are long, complicated and often frustrating experiences. Because of this, because of the time it often takes to get justice, because of severe court congestion that can delay a trial for years, and other problems in the civil justice system, people and businesses are increasingly turning to alternative dispute resolution (ADR) to resolve consumer disputes.

ADR is intended to bring access to justice in a less expensive, faster and more people-friendly process than traditional litigation. Here are some answers to commonly asked questions about ADR:

What Kind of Programs Are Part of ADR?

There are two primary types of ADR procedures:

Mediation. Mediation occurs when a neutral third party who has been trained in dispute resolution sits down with disputing parties in an informal setting to help them "settle the case." Often, mediators help parties achieve a mutual compromise with the added benefit that lawyers often do not need to be hired. Mediation, unlike litigation, is not an adversarial process and is particularly valuable for disputes between people who have ongoing relationships such as neighbors, consumers and business people. Also, the mediator cannot compel you or the other side to settle. Thus, in many mediations, there is little to lose but possibly a lot to gain.

Arbitration. The other principal tool of ADR is *arbitration.* Arbitration proceedings are like informal trials. After each side has presented their case to the arbitrator, a decision will be made in much the same way as a judge or jury reaches a verdict.

Depending on the agreement of the parties, the arbitrator's decision may be *binding* or *nonbinding.* If it is nonbinding, the matter could be brought to a court of law. An arbitrator's nonbinding decision may be admittable in court. If the arbitration is binding, the case is over. If a party ordered in the binding arbitration to pay money refuses, the arbitration decision can be converted into a court judgment and enforced as such.

How Much Does ADR Cost?

This is an important question that should be thoroughly explored before deciding to pursue your dispute through ADR. In litigation, other than minor filing fees, the use of judges, courts and other court personnel is free, since the courts are part of the government and supported by taxes. ADR facilities, on the other hand, support themselves by charging the participants fees (some ADR facilities also receive grants). In addition, the parties themselves have to pay the fees charged by the mediator or arbitrator.

ADR can be expensive. In California for example, many ADR proceedings use retired judges who charge the parties $200 an hour for their services. Happily, many ADR programs are not this expensive. For example, the American Arbitration Association has a sliding fee schedule. For example, as of this writing, if the dispute is worth less than $25,000, the fee is $300 plus paying the arbitrator or mediator approximately $500 per day, which is split by the parties. (The charge will be higher for disputes involving more money.)

Still, even at these "cut rates," a one-day arbitration can cost *each party* $400 or $500. Many larger communities have neighborhood dispute resolution centers who charge little or nothing for their services. In addition, if the case is referred to ADR by a court, there may be no charge. Moreover, ADR operated under the auspices of private associations such as the Better Business Bureau is usually quite affordable.

(For more information on local ADR dispute centers, contact the ABA Section on Dispute Resolution, 1800 M St., N.W., Washington, DC 20036; telephone number (202) 331-2258.

How Do I Get Involved With ADR?

Generally, there are three ways to invoke ADR:

By Contract. Increasingly, business contracts are utilizing "arbitration clauses" in their contracts to compel you to resort to ADR if a problem arises. (Be sure you understand these terms completely and the costs that could be associated with such an arbitration before agreeing to an arbitration clause.)

By Agreement. When a consumer dispute arises, the parties can agree to mediate or arbitrate rather than go to court.

By Court Order. As stated above, some courts refer cases to ADR.

What Are the Advantages of ADR?

Many people like ADR because of the speed and the fact that lawyers may not be involved. (You can use a lawyer in ADR if you wish and you may want to if the stakes are high.) The matter is also private; there will not be a public record. Mediation, in particular, allows people to resolve their problems while maintaining a good relationship with each other.

Are There Any Disadvantages?

Yes. ADR works best with participants who have relatively equal power. If you are up against a major institution, such as an insurance company, you may be bowled over by their clout. After all, in arbitration you don't have the right to discovery or the ability to go to a judge and force your adversary to play by the rules, as you do in litigation. Also, as stated earlier, the expense (absent attorneys' fees) can be higher than traditional litigation, since you are paying for access to justice.

ADMINISTRATIVE PROCESSES

If you believe you have been harmed by a bank, a credit card company, have suffered discrimination based on race, gender, disability or etc., or have any other consumer complaint, you can report the offender to the appropriate administrative agency.

The procedures after your report will depend on what the administrative agency decides to do with your case. Sometimes the agency will pursue the matter and you will be a witness. At other times, it will give you permission to sue in your own name. Or, they may conduct mediations to help you and the other side resolve the dispute.

The most significant benefit of pursuing the administrative law route is that you may be able to have the government enforce your rights for you—and on the government's dime. Also, a wrongdoer may be more likely to make amends when faced with the power and financial might of a government agency than an individual, who may not be able to afford an attorney or court costs.

For more consumer information on how a particular administrative proceeding would be conducted, contact the appropriate administrative agency.

4

AVOIDING SHARP PRACTICES
IN THE MARKETPLACE

The fact that consumers have greater power than ever before does not mean that there aren't pitfalls to watch out for. In fact, your "caveat emptor" radar should always be about the business of looking out for sharp practices and start red lights blinking and sirens wailing in your head at the first sign that a deal is not kosher. You should also be on the lookout for perfectly legal practices (refund policies, etc.) which limit your rights as a consumer.

The unfortunate fact of the matter is that there are a lot of crooks and fast operators out there hoping to take advantage of you. Consumer fraud, quick sale schemes—even legal marketing practices—can cost you. Understanding the nature of these "dangers" and how to spot and avoid them can not only save you a lot of money but also time and tremendous aggravation.

This chapter will cover three areas of concern: fraud, marketing schemes which are legal but to be avoided, and some of the "tricks of the trade" of high pressure sales that can induce you to buy when you don't really want to.

CONSUMER FRAUD

Fraud literally costs consumers billions of dollars a year. As just one example, the Alliance Against Fraud in Telemarketing has estimated that telephone scams alone will cost consumers more than $10 billion a year by the end of the decade. That's more than $1 million an hour!

Fraud can be found in just about any industry, ranging from home repair scams to security cons to time-tested criminal schemes like the bank examiner fiasco. Often, the people who are victimized are elderly, who tend to be more trusting and vulnerable. Also at risk are people looking for the "unbelievable deal" or for the proverbial but nonexistent "free lunch." Most of the time such people get less than they bargained for. However, even legitimate sounding offers can be bogus. The truth of the matter is that some fraudulent operators are becoming so sophisticated that *anyone* can fall prey.

The following is a sampling of some of the most common scams:

Medical Quackery

Quackery is the promotion of a medical remedy that has not been proven to work. People who are ill can be especially vulnerable due to their natural desire to have restored health. Crooks know this and seek to take advantage of their victim's desperation.

At best, quackery can cost you money spent for a worthless product. At worst, quackery can cost you your life if it keeps you from seeking proper medical care. (Having a family doctor to discuss issues of health care with can go a long way toward defeating even the most sophisticated quack.)

There are several warning signs of quackery:

- Promises of a miracle cure
- Promises of immediate results
- Allegations that doctors don't want you to know
- Excited advertisements of newly-discovered secret herbs, powders or machines
- Special out-of-the-country clinics offering cures not permitted in the USA

Quacks often target people with ailments that are life threatening or which cause significant emotional distress, such as people with cancer, arthritis, impotence or obesity. There is an antidote, however—your family doctor or pharmacist. Thus, if you are pitched a new miracle cure discovered among the indigenous people of the Amazon that will restore hair, virility and make your teeth white while aiding digestion, give your doctor or pharmacist a call. If they wouldn't buy it, you shouldn't either.

If you believe you have been approached by a quack, contact your local police department or state department of consumer affairs.

Pyramid Schemes

Pyramid schemes are a form of con game that makes suckers out of participants and induces them to break criminal laws. Here's how a pyramid typically works:

The mastermind offers "distributorships," "shares" or other such memberships. In order to participate, the investor must deposit money into the plan. For their money, each member is allowed to sell other memberships for the same price, with the promise that they will eventually receive a financial return from future investors into the game. (For example the mastermind may keep half of the money and distribute the rest among those that he or she first brought into the scheme.) Then, each of the new members sell memberships, with the money being distributed to those who came into the scheme before them, creating a chain of sales that looks like a pyramid (thus the name) with few at the top making a lot of money and many at the bottom losing it.

The scam is sold as a "can't lose" money-maker to participants. Often, the crooked nature of the scheme is masked by involving a product kit which may come for the price of the investment. Some people who get into the scheme early can make money (if the scam is run "honestly"). However, later participants are likely to lose their money as the steam runs out of the game and fewer people participate.

Pyramid schemes are against the law. If you participate in one you not only risk your money but your freedom. Moreover, many victims of pyramids are urged by the operators to bring their friends into the scheme "as a favor." When they lose money you may lose the relationship.

Pyramids schemes, which are illegal, are sometimes confused with multi-level marketing companies (MLM) such as Amway, which are legitimate. Like pyramid schemes, MLM companies offer their participants sales incentives for bringing people into the company (a process known as recruitment) by allowing them to earn commissions from the sales made by those they recruit into the company. If these commissions are based on *actual sales*, the MLM is probably legal. (For example, the venerable Fuller Brush Company is now operated as an MLM enterprise.) However, if the MLM pays money based on successful recruitment, it probably isn't legal. Thus, before signing up for a MLM company, be sure to make sure that it is not a pyramid by contacting your state Attorney General's office. You should also take the time to make sure the product is legitimate, too, since many MLM companies offer products that are, to put it politely, out of the mainstream.

Home Improvement Frauds

Each year many people are bilked out of their hard-earned money through home improvement frauds. Building scams involve everything from roofing to aluminum siding to driveway repairs. Typically, a salesperson will approach your door, and say something like, "We are a roofing company with crews in the area. We are offering free roof inspections and discounts on repairs to keep our crews busy."

Not surprisingly, the "inspector" finds something terribly wrong and you are quickly pressured into signing a contract, always with a substantial down payment. Sometimes the contractor keeps the money and never starts the work. At other times, work is begun but never completed. Or, the work will be fully performed but in such a slipshod manner that it is virtually worthless. Unfortunately, you may not become aware of the problem for months, by which time the crooks have moved on to another city.

It is never a good idea to buy building contractor services from a door-to-door salesperson. Rather, you should get competitive bids from well-known and respected contractors. (See

Chapter 12.) However, if you are approached and are interested in using the company (all door-to-door building contractors are not crooks), be sure to ask for the contractor's license number and call your state's licensing board and ask if the company is legitimate. For safety's sake, don't let anyone into your home unless they have credentials. Also, ask for an address and telephone number of the home office and call. Ask for a list of satisfied customers and call to make sure they are legitimate. Finally, ask for a little time to decide so you can do your investigation. If anything appears amiss, call the police.

Telemarketing Fraud

Telephone fraud is a multi-million dollar business that involves selling or misrepresenting products over the telephone. Of course, not every telephone solicitor is a phony. Thus, it may be difficult to separate the legitimate solicitors from those who are crooks.

The Alliance Against Fraud in Telemarketing has published nine tip-offs that may indicate a caller is a crook. They are:

High Pressure Sales Tactics. If the telemarketer pressures you to buy, or won't let you say no, hang up.

Insistence On an Immediate Decision. Con artists often insist that you must make an immediate decision. And they always have a seemingly good reason.

The Offer Sounds to Good to Be True. It isn't always easy to spot false claims, because good telecrooks often mix truth with half truths and lies. However, if an offer seems more than can be believed—it probably is.

A Request For Your Credit Card Number For Any Reason Other Than to Make a Purchase. Swindlers often ask victims for credit card numbers for "purposes of identification" or "verification" or some other nice sounding but illegitimate purpose, such as showing good faith so you can be awarded a prize. Once they have your number, they will use it—and not for the purpose they stated.

An Offer to Send Someone to Your House to Pick Up Money.
If they are in that big a rush, be wary.

**A Statement That You Are Getting Something For Free;
Followed By a Requirement That You Pay.** For example, if you
are asked only to pay for shipping and handling (so please give
them your credit card number), it is probably not legitimate.

An Investment Opportunity That Is Pitched As Risk-Free.
There's no such thing as a risk-free investment, with the possible
exception of investments guaranteed by the full faith and credit
of the United States.

A Reluctance to Provide Written Information or References.
Their failure to provide references or verify information should
be a clear warning sign.

**A Suggestion That You Should Make a Purchase Based On
Trust.** As a former president once said in a different context,
"trust, but verify."

Telemarketing is a growing business with tremendous opportunities for fraud and abuse. Thus, be on the lookout for fast
operators. Be especially wary of telemarketing involving prize
offers, penny stocks, business-to-business products, magazine
subscriptions, credit repair, travel scams and work-at-home
business opportunities.

Financial Investment Scams

There are so many forms of business scams that they are too
numerous to detail here. According to the Economic Crime
Project of the National District Attorney's Association, tens of
thousands of people are cheated every year by con artists prom-
ising financial opportunities.

In difficult economic times, such offers can be especially
tempting. Your job as an investor in a business opportunity is to
make sure the deal is above-board. If a lot of money is at stake,
hire a business lawyer and/or a CPA knowledgeable in the type
of opportunity you are investigating. While you are checking
into the proposal, be sure to look out for the following:

- Undue pressure to sign quickly
- A demand that you pay a large sum of money before you can investigate
- Promises of unusually high profits
- Evasive answers from sales personnel
- Unwillingness to disclose documents
- Unwillingness to put verbal promises in writing

A lot of people are cheated while looking for a legitimate business opportunity. A little wariness can keep you from being one of them.

Deceptive Advertising

Another form of wrongful conduct to watch out for is deceptive advertising. Advertisements are designed to get you to want to buy. Most of these tactics are legitimate—at least legally. However, some forms of advertisement are improper or illegal. Here is a sampling:

- Prices advertised at one level but actually charged at a higher level
- Surcharges that are not disclosed in the ad
- Fees that are not disclosed in the ad
- Mandatory add-ons that are not disclosed in the ad
- Not having the product advertised unless the ad specifically stated that there was a limited quantity or identified the products to be sold (for example, a few cars offered at a special price which are identified by license and identification number)

If you believe you have been the intended or actual victim of a scam, do something about it. Here's who you should contact:

The FTC. To obtain relief from deceptive sales practices, report the seller to the FTC. It can order the seller to remedy the situation and to stop unlawful activity.

The Police. Your police department will have a bunco squad to look into fraud and con games.

The District Attorney or State Attorney General. Both will usually have personnel who focus on scams.

The Post Office. If the information given as part of the scam was communicated to you by mail, or asks for return money by mail, the Post Office should be notified so it can investigate.

Your State Department of Consumer Affairs. It is their job to protect you. If you believe you have been bilked, especially by a business, give your local office a call.

Your State Contractor's Licensing Board. If your problem involves a builder, let the Contracting Board know about it.

The State Department of Real Estate. If your problem involves a real estate broker or a mortgage loan, this agency should be able to help.

There are a lot of other local, state and federal agencies that help people who have been cheated. But the list above is a good place to start. If they can't help you, ask them to refer you to other sources of assistance.

SHARP BUSINESS PRACTICES

Every business practice you should watch out for isn't illegal. Some are perfectly legitimate but can end up costing you money you didn't want to spend. Here's a sampling:

Negative-Acceptance Contracts

Most consumer purchases are made when the buyer takes positive action to make a purchase. Thus, if you want a new suit, you go to the store, shop, pick out one you like and lay your money (or credit card) down. Likewise, if you shop by catalog, you must send away for your purchase or call and make it by telephone.

However, there are some situations where you buy a product when you take *no action*. These are known as negative acceptance contracts. Here's how the negative contract works:

- You are induced to sign up with a purchasing club, typically a book club, record club or credit card buying club, with offers such as 10 books for 10 cents, or other such buying incentives.
- You obtain the tremendous bargain by signing up for the club. Typically, you will have to buy a specified number of full-price items to fulfill your obligation under the contract terms.
- Every month, you will receive a catalogue of items from which you can decide to make a purchase. There will also be a purchase-of-the-month listed.
- If you take no action by a specific date, you will automatically receive the purchase-of-the-month. In other words, *doing nothing constitutes an automatic order.* This is the negative acceptance. Or, if you buy other items and don't specifically checkoff the form for the company not to send the purchase-of-the-month, you will still receive it.
- The only way not to receive the purchase of the month is if you positively check the appropriate spot on the purchase form stating you don't want it and then mail it to the company.

It's easy to see how negative-acceptance contracts can cost you money you do not intend to spend. Instead of taking action to buy something, you can take no action and still buy something. (For instance, if you forget to send the form declining the purchase.) Moreover, many of these clubs charge high shipping and handling fees, which can cost you extra money.

That is not to say you should not do business with a negative-acceptance type company. They are perfectly legal and many people like them because of the convenience and the fact that the clubs sometimes offer valuable discounts, especially to customers who purchase frequently. However, you should know what you are buying into before you sign on the dotted line.

Succumbing to High Pressure Sales Tactics

Many businesses use high pressure tactics to get people to buy. This is legal, unless the tactics amount to fraud or actual duress.

Salespeople know that the key to high pressure sales success is psychology. For example, some selling tactics involve getting the customer into a "yes" mode. Thus, the sales person will ask questions which elicit a yes response. For example, if you are looking to purchase a new stereo, you might be asked:

> **Salesperson:** Does your old stereo permit you to record off of the CD?
> **You:** Yes.
> **Salesperson:** Is this a feature you want in your next stereo?
> **You:** Yes.
> **Salesperson:** Are there other features you want?
> **You:** Yes. I would like to be able to dub cassettes.
> **Salesperson:** So, the stereo you want should have a CD and be able to dub cassettes.
> **You:** Yes.
> **Salesperson:** Great! I have just the stereo you are looking for and it's on sale! We have it in stock. I could have a stock boy load it in your trunk if you'd like.
> **You:** OK. Sure.

Of course, the sales pitch would be more sophisticated and detailed than the one depicted above but you get the idea. The theory is that once the customer is in a yes mode, he or she will be more likely to go along than stop and say, "No, I want to shop around some more."

Another high pressure tactic involves group psychology, where the customer is induced to buy by an artificially-created buying frenzy created among a group kept in a remote location. If I may be permitted a personal anecdote, the following is a true story of such a sales pitch I endured when I was in my early twenties:

> My parents and I took a vacation to Las Vegas. When we arrived, we were handed a coupon offering us free tickets to a show if we owned our own homes (which they did and I did) and would listen to a sales presentation about some land in Arizona that was going to be developed into a "vacation paradise." In order to qualify, we had to remain for the entire presentation.

(*Note:* Our desire to obtain "something for nothing" was used as the foot-in-the-door to get us in a situation where we could be induced to make a purchase. Today, I would not bite.)

> When we arrived at the designated time, we and about fifty prospects were herded into a room and, in a very friendly way, directed to tables. A

salesperson was assigned to each table who began to ask us about ourselves in a very conversational, agreeable way. We were offered free food and all began to chat and get relaxed.

(To "soften us up" we were filled with good food and put off our guard by the nice, friendly salesman, who seemed so interested in us and our lives. Of course, what he was really doing was breaking down our defenses and sizing us up for the kill.)

After about 10 minutes, a nice, trustworthy-looking man with gray hair took a podium at the front of the room, welcomed us to this exciting opportunity and told us our show tickets would be handed out at the end of the presentation. He said he wanted to show us a film. The room darkened, and Will Rodgers, Jr. appeared on horseback to pitch the amazing vacation community that was being developed by the company.

(One way to get people to buy is to have a celebrity pitch the deal. Many people respond to celebrity endorsements because they feel like they know the celebrity as a friend and are thus put off their guard. But note, celebrity endorsements are *paid for*— often at a very high price. Thus, the presence or absence of a celebrity endorsement should never be a reason to buy.)

After the film ended, the high pressure sales tactics began. The salesman at our table began to ask questions, designed to make us say yes. If we said no, he immediately asked us why we would say no, and seek to overcome every objection, until he could get another yes answer. All of our objections had an answer. The effect was to make us feel dumb if we didn't see the marvelous opportunity we were being offered.

After about five minutes, I decided to opt out of this. The only thing I would say was "I'm not interested." Then he asked what he had done wrong that I did not appreciate what was being offered. I simply repeated, "Nothing. I'm just not interested." He asked if it was the money because he could offer low monthly terms, to which I replied, "I'm not interested." After a few minutes of this, I was getting angry and the man was getting furious. He went and got his boss who smiled, sat down at the table and asked me what the problem was. I said, "There's no problem. I'm simply not interested." The boss repeated the kinds of questions his underling had posed, to which I replied, "I'm not interested." Finally, he told me if I wanted to leave I could but I would not get the free ticket. I told him, no, I was entitled to the free ticket so I would stay. He left the table in a red-faced fury.

Then, one of the salesmen rang a bell, and announced, "Salesmen, lot 42 has been sold. It is no longer available!" The entire sales force burst into applause. This was repeated every five minutes or so, with a different lot supposedly having been sold.

> I was being left alone now, and I looked around the room. Everywhere sales people and customers were involved in intense discussions. I could literally feel the emotions in the room rising. People were getting excited. Then, the bell rang again and another lot was announced as having been sold. This time, the buyers were asked to stand. We were all asked to give them a big round of applause. The purchasers stood there beaming.
>
> This continued for about thirty minutes with several parcels being sold. I have often wondered what those people did with what I assume is now their worthless desert land.

Note the psychology that was applied. Everyone wants to be liked and receive approval and to be able to get in on a good thing. The sales people played to these natural desires by staging phony sales. Thus, the emotions in the room were raised as they tried to create a buying frenzy, where people purchased based on the emotion of the moment rather than being given a chance to reflect on the sale or to decide whether they even wanted vacation property in Arizona.

This experience may have been an extreme example of high pressure sales but the approach was similar to most high pressure sales tactics. Simply put, the high pressure salesperson tries to make you feel good for being so smart to spot such a good deal. If that doesn't work, they will try to make you feel bad for not going along with the pitch. Feeling bad, or guilty, worried you'll miss out on a deal or on the defensive should never be the reason you decide to buy. Quite the contrary, being made to feel that way is a good reason not to buy.

Happily, high pressure sales pitches are easy to defeat if you realize you do not owe the salesperson a sale, much less an answer to questions or statements. So, when in doubt, simply say, "I'm not interested." (You may enjoy an added bonus of watching the salesperson's face turn beet-red.) Also, if the sale involves an installment payment plan, *the law provides that you have three days within which to change your mind.* If you do fall prey to high pressure sales and you have such an escape clause, be sure to use it if you change your mind.

(*Note*: If you sign a contract, the fact that high pressure sales tactics were used will not release you from your obligation, unless the salesperson engaged in illegal conduct. Many people have found this out the hard way when they were successfully sued, after they refused to make payments.)

Sales Gimmicks

There are other sales gimmicks you should be aware of. They include:

Bait and Switch. As the name implies, a bait and switch scheme gets you into a store based on an advertisement of a very good bargain. Once in the store, you are "switched" to some other piece of merchandise which ends up giving you less value or causes you to pay more than you had planned. Bait and switch schemes are illegal but they happen all the time.

Loss Leaders. Loss leaders are specially marked-down items which are offered to get you in the store in the hope that you will impulse buy enough other merchandise to more than make up for the low price of the item that induced you to go to the store in the first place. The cure for the loss leader is to only purchase the item you came for, assuming it is a legitimate value and it is something you really want to buy.

Deceptive Packaging. Some items are packaged to look like more than they really are. So, always look behind the veneer to make sure you are getting your money's worth.

The Phony List Price. Unscrupulous retailers will say they sell an item for a higher price than they really do so you will think you are receiving a bargain. Consumer activism can catch this little maneuver by comparison price shopping at other outlets. If the list price is indeed a phony, contact your state department of consumer affairs.

There are many other sales techniques and sleazy business practices existing in the marketplace and new ones are being invented all of the time. The key to not becoming a victim is to stay in charge of your own buying. When you are in the market, you should do your homework so you will have sufficient product knowledge with which to make an intelligent decision. You should be the one to decide whether the price is fair. By staying in control of your own purchasing agenda, you are less likely to be taken in by high pressure, deception or the sales presentation.

Now, let's take a quick look at some of the legal rights you enjoy when you shop and when you buy.

5

YOUR RIGHTS
WHEN YOU SHOP

This chapter will describe your legal rights in the market-place. Some of these have already been touched upon in previous chapters, such as the right not to be the victim of fraud or deceptive advertising, which was addressed in the last chapter. In this chapter, we will complete the discussion. We will describe how you obtain information about products and services, the issue of *warranties*, both express and implied, and how to decide whether to buy an extended express warranty, known as a service contract. Extra-legal resources that can be called on to help with consumer problems will also be described.

A CONSUMER'S BILL OF RIGHTS

As a buyer of products, you have rights. Some of these, like warranties, are found in the bedrock of law. Other rights stem from basic concepts of equity and fair play. All should be followed every time you enter into a commercial transaction.

You Have the Right to Know What You Are Buying

That seems elementary, but it isn't. Too many people buy without fully knowing the score. For example, look at the people who bought the desert land (described in the last chapter) based on a film and high pressure. They had never even seen the land they were buying!

Buying based on anything but solid, reliable information can cost you in many ways. It may result in your being cheated. More often, purchases made in the dark will increase the likelihood of your making a mistake. For example, you might buy a product that does not perform as you had hoped, not because it was poorly constructed but because you did not know enough to know that it would not fit your needs. Or, you might end up buying too much of a good thing—a product that has more features than you will ever use, features you pay for, features that are nothing less than a waste of your hard-earned money.

Such mistakes can be virtually eliminated by holding off your purchase until you have a solid grasp of the information you need to make an intelligent decision. Happily, there are an abundance of sources of consumer information to assist you about various products and services.

Consumer Reports Magazine. Perhaps the best overall source of consumer information is *Consumers Reports*. The company that puts out this information is not afraid of stepping on anyone's toes because they refuse advertising or other financial support from industry sources. Moreover, the people who work and test the products and services covered each month in the magazine are experts and do not have the wool pulled over their eyes.

Each month, *Consumer Reports* covers many of the most common purchases you and your family can make. One month it may be television sets, answering machines and vacuum cleaners. The next it may be automobiles, personal computers and popcorn makers. What sets *Consumer Reports* above the pack is their product comparisons, in which they obtain and comparison test major and minor brand names and report to the reader on issues ranging from price to ease-of-use to reliability and, if relevant, safety. These comparisons also offer the consumer valuable information they need to understand if they are to make an informed purchase.

There are few products or services that the magazine has not tackled at one time or another. Your local library should have back issues. You can find a copy of the magazine at your nearest newsstand, or if you would like to subscribe, call *Consumer Reports* at (800) 288-7898.

Government Entities. The government can also be an excellent source of consumer information. For example, if you're in the market for insurance, your state Department of Insurance publishes consumer guides to help you. They may also publish consumer complaint comparisons and other important data to help you compare insurance companies. (See Chapter 11.) Or, if you want to learn more about buying good, nutritious food for your family, the U.S. Department of Agriculture can send you very valuable guides concerning food groups, nutrition, how to get good food value, how to read food labels and how to handle food safely. Other helpful government entities will be described in later chapters as we discuss specific products and services.

Nonprofit Groups. There are many nonprofit consumer organizations who assist consumers. These nonprofit organizations can be especially helpful regarding issues of safety. One is Consumer's Union, which publishes *Consumer Reports*. Consumer's Union has a wide list of valuable consumer books that can assist you. (For a catalogue list, call (914) 378-2000. Public Citizen, a Washington, D.C.-based group, is another invaluable source of information. For example, the Public Citizen Health Research Group puts out a newsletter, called *Health Letter*, which contains invaluable and up-to-date information on issues and topics important to your health and to obtaining quality health care. Public Citizen Health Research Group can be contacted at (202) 833-3000.

Trade Associations. Trade associations are created to protect and promote the interests of their members. However, they also provide valuable consumer information to consumers about the products (or services) its members peddle. The information will be generic; that is, it will not be product specific, but rather will cover the ins-and-outs of what to look for when purchasing the kind of product without going into the differences among the many brands that may be on the market. Many also have 800 numbers to call if you have any questions.

Books. There are a lot of books on the market which instruct consumers on how to make smart purchases. Your local book store or library will have a wide variety of these, ranging from issues of the law to buying real property and automobiles. For information about some of these titles, see Appendix 6 (Bibliography).

Retailers. Retailers also offer important information. Sometimes they have pamphlets that describe their products and services. Salespeople are also an important source of information. If you are shopping for an item, you may want to take notes when talking to different salespeople. Not only will you learn a lot about the type of product or service you are interested in buying, but the pros and cons of different brands and models as well. Manufacturers also frequently offer equivalent information.

You Have the Right to Good Value

Every time you purchase a product or service, you should receive *value.* That is not the same thing as cheap or inexpensive. Sometimes the lowest-priced items also have the poorest value. What that term does mean is that you receive a product or service of appropriate quality for the price you paid. Or to put it another way, value means buying a quality product at a fair price.

How do you judge value? It can be that satisfied feeling of getting your money's worth. Or, it may be as simple as being able to "not think about" the product or service once purchased because it "works." In this context, value can be expressed in having the promises made to you kept or problems satisfied.

If you believe you did not receive value, you should speak up and complain. This is more important than just receiving personal satisfaction (which is certainly a worthwhile goal). Complaining about poor values also helps the system because, when combined with the complaints of other dissatisfied customers, it can stimulate needed change in a product's manufacture or presentation. Moreover, if you receive poor value and suffer in silence, you reward shoddy practices and thereby encourage them, since there is no penalty to be paid. It also punishes ethical retailers and manufacturers because they receive no benefit for the added time, expense and effort that they have invested in bringing value to the marketplace.

You Have the Right to Good Service

It used to be said, "The customer is always right." Unfortunately, many enterprises seem to have forgotten that truism. But you shouldn't, and you should not shop at stores or contract with service providers that have.

What is good service? Service that:

- Treats you with respect and with the knowledge that you are the source of the provider's income
- Tells you the truth
- Does not try to get your money by high pressure tactics or by pulling the wool over your eyes
- Gives you the benefit of the doubt if there is a dispute
- Patiently explains the reasons you are not going to be accommodated if that is to happen (this should only happen if there's a good and substantial reason)
- Is never rude
- Walks the extra mile to give you satisfaction

You probably have your own definitions of good service to add to this list. By insisting on receiving such respectful treatment, you will be doing your part to make the marketplace a better, more consumer-oriented arena.

You Have the Right to a Warranty

When you buy a product or service, you have the right to a warranty, or to know that you are not receiving one.

There are basically two kinds of warranties: *express warranties* and *implied warranties*. Here's the scoop on both:

Express Warranties. An express warranty is a promise to you that any problems you experience with the product or service will be remedied pursuant to the terms of the promise. The terms of the warranty are enforceable in a court of law because the promises you received in the warranty are part and parcel of the contract of purchase—they are part of what you bargained and paid for when you made the purchase.

It is very important that you understand the terms of the warranty, since all warranties may not be the same. For example, be sure and find out the following:

How long is the warranty? The longer the warranty, the better your protection.

How broad is the warranty? It is very important to look at the "fine print" of warranties because sometimes they offer less than they might appear to. For example, assume a warranty for a refrigerator offers five years of protection. Is that for the entire product or only part of it, such as, say, the compressor? Also note that warranties often offer broader protection for the cost of parts than they do labor. Why? Because the cost of labor is often the most expensive part of a repair.

How is the warranty backed up? A company can offer a warranty from here to infinity but if it is not in business, the warranty can be framed and hung on the wall for all of the good it will do you. Thus, determining the reliability of the warranty provider is important in judging the value you will receive with the warranty.

How is the warranty fulfilled? Convenience may be an important issue when judging a warranty. For example, if you buy a television, is the warranty a replacement warranty or a repair warranty? (A replacement warranty gives you the right to a new television if yours malfunctions during the term of the warranty. A repair warranty would require the warranty provider to give you a free repair.) That's not all. If the warranty is a repair warranty, where would the repair take place: In the store? In a distant repair station? In your home? Who pays if shipping is necessary? Also, how long would the repair take? And what about the repairs themselves, are they warranted? The answer to these questions may be important in your buying decision.

Some express warranties are required of one or both parties by law. For example, many states require the seller of real property to disclose all conditions of the property that could materially affect the sale. The seller thereafter warrants that there are no other adverse conditions to worry about. If there are undisclosed conditions, the buyer can bring a lawsuit for damages.

Most warranties are offered with the product "free of charge."

(This is a misnomer, of course, since the cost of the warranty to the manufacturer or retailer is included in the price.) Many people are also interested in extended warranties, commonly known as service contracts. In fact, so many people buy service contracts that it is a profitable industry separate and apart from the sale of merchandise.

A service contract is an express warranty that you buy in addition to the warranty that "comes" with the product. Service contracts may be offered by the retailer or the manufacturer, or, on occasion, as with automobile service contracts, by companies that were not part of the original sales transaction. If you are interested in buying a service contract, be sure to keep the following in mind:

- What is the warranty that comes with the price of purchase? If the warranty is for a relatively long period, you may not need to extend it.
- What is the price? A service contract can add significantly to the cost of the product and may put you over the amount you had budgeted for the purchase.
- What is the likelihood that the product will require service? If a product is unlikely to need service, a service contract is a waste of money. On the other hand, if the product is one that can often suffer service problems, the opposite may be true. (Knowing the likelihood of requiring service is one of the things you should look for when doing your product research.)
- How expensive is a repair likely to be if the item malfunctions "out of warranty?" Repair work can cost nearly as much as buying a new product. This being so, a service contract may be a good value since it assures that you will not have to put out more money on repairs or a replacement product during the term of the warranty.
- Who would provide the service? You need to be assured that repairs will be performed by a reliable source. Thus, this question can be key.
- Are there any additional costs if you buy, such as a deductible? Some extended warranties are limited; that is, they don't cover all possible costs of repair. This can make a difference in your decision-making process.

- Can you purchase the contract at a later date? Retail salespersons often push service contracts because they are paid a commission for the sale. However, you may not need to buy the service contract at the point of purchase. That may make a difference in your decision to extend the warranty when you are buying the product.
- Does the service contract cover normal maintenance services, such as cleaning and inspection? Often, service contracts are sold on the basis that their cost also includes cleaning and maintenance. This can make a service contract a good deal—if you take advantage of this service (which many people do not do).

Many retailers and product manufacturers push hard for their customers to purchase service contracts. That is not because the products are shoddy, but because service contracts can be sources of good profits for the companies offering them. Many consumer advocates recommend against taking service contracts because they can be expensive and may never be utilized. However, the only one who can really determine whether the peace of mind and potential savings is worth the price is you, based on your individual circumstances and the terms and price of the contract that is being offered.

Implied Warranties. When you make a purchase, you also receive implied warranties. A warranty is implied when it is not directly made a part of the bargaining but is legally held to exist by the very nature of the business transaction through operation of law.

One of the most important implied warranties is the warranty of "merchantability." The warranty of merchantability simply states that the product is fit for the purpose for which it was designed and sold. Thus, in order to be merchantable, a lawn mower must cut grass, a refrigerator must cool food, and a light bulb must light. Part of the warranty also has to do with safety. If the lawn mower is safe if used properly, it will pass the merchantability test. However, if it is likely to cut off your foot, it will not be merchantable. Violation of this warranty can give rise to redress, ranging from a right to your money back to a lawsuit for all reasonable damages you can prove you sustained, depending on the circumstances.

There is also the implied warranty of "fitness for a particular purpose." If you have told the sales person that you want to use a product for a specified and particular purpose and you *rely on the salesperson's expertise* in selecting a model aimed at fulfilling that particular purpose, the law will imply the existence of a warranty. For example:

- If you tell a salesperson that you want to buy a cooking appliance to smoke the salmon you catch, and:
- He sells you a barbecue that he describes as also being designed to smoke meat, and:
- The barbecue, in fact, is incapable of smoking meat. Then, you are entitled to a refund or other recourse (for example, the extra cost it would take to make the barbecue capable of smoking meat) because the product, while merchantable (it barbecues), did not meet the particular purpose for which you bought it (it does not smoke meat).

Another important implied warranty is the "warranty of good faith and fair dealing." Once parties are in a contractual relationship, each party owes the other a duty of treating them fairly and in good faith in all matters dealing with the performance of the contract. (This does not apply before the contract is entered into when the bargaining for terms is deemed at arm's length, nor does it apply to the "salesman's art.")

Failure to abide by this implied contractual duty can give rise to a lawsuit based on breach of contract or tort. This can be particularly important for consumers who seek to enforce insurance contracts.

"As Is" Purchases. The law recognizes that parties sometimes contract with each other in such a manner that they intend that there be no warranties created, whether express or implied. This is usually known as an *As Is* sale.

An As Is sale returns the consumer back to a strict *caveat emptor* transaction since what you see (and perhaps don't see) is what you get. An As Is sale extinguishes any warranties that apply and any rights for which you would otherwise have to seek redress should the product not perform as expected or should there be any defects which you were not aware of when making the purchase. For example, if you buy a used car sold as is and it turns out to have bad brakes, that fact cannot become the basis of an action for breach of contract or breach of warranty. (This does not mean, however, that you can be defrauded simply because the sale is made As Is. Thus, if the car with bad brakes was sold based partially on the sales person's representation that new brakes had just been installed in the car, when in fact the brakes were old, you would still have an action for breach of contract or fraud even if you made the purchase As Is.)

As Is purchases are risky because you are giving up important legal rights. However, the return is often a very low price. Thus, you may decide to take the risk, especially if you are "good with your hands" and can repair any problems that arise yourself. (Many people buy products As Is, such as cars or houses, at a price well below market rates, fix them up and sell them for a profit.) However, if you do not have the time or expertise to make your own repairs, buying As Is may not be worth the bother or the risk.

Warranties and your rights under them are an important part of any buying decision. Thus, before committing to a purchase, be sure you understand all of your rights under the terms of the purchase and the ease by which you would enforce them. Also keep in mind the reputation of the warrantor (the person or entity giving the warranty) to make sure that you would receive performance in the event you have to rely on the promises made in the warranty.

You Have the Right to Have Complaints Taken Seriously

Complaints by consumers are very important to the proper functioning of our market-based economy. Complaints allow consumers to receive equitable treatment in the marketplace without having to seek redress in court. Complaints tell business managers if something is wrong with a product or the manner in which they do business.

Good complaining skills should help you solve problems without resort to court, alternate dispute resolution or other formal dispute resolving mechanisms, which were discussed in earlier chapters. Moreover, good complaining can provide a solid foundation should you need to resort to more formal remedies. (For tips on effective complaining, see Chapter 2.)

If a business does not have time for your complaints or treats them with disregard or disdain, you should complain to an appropriate government agency, such as the Department of Consumer Affairs, to a "higher up" like a corporate headquarters, or to a business group, such as the Better Business Bureau or local Chamber of Commerce. If appropriate, you can take the matter to a licensing board, such as the State Board of Realtors or State Bar Association, although they usually can't get your money back for you.

If you are in doubt where to turn to if your complaints are not taken seriously, try one or more of these sources:

Federal Information Centers. FICs can direct you to the right federal agency, if appropriate, through which to seek redress. To find the one in your state, look in the telephone book under federal government, or call 800 information at (800) 555-1212 and ask for the number. If that doesn't work, contact your congressperson's local office and ask a staff member to get the telephone number for you.

Your Local or State Department of Consumer Affairs. The number will be in your telephone book under city or state government.

Your Government Representative. Often, your city council person or your state or federal representative will have staff to help direct you to the best source of consumer redress.

Media Ombudsman. In larger cities, some television and radio stations have consumer ombudsmen who help consumers solve problems and then report on it on their news or consumer-oriented programs. If any of your media outlets have such programs, go for it. Never underestimate the power of the press.

In Part 2, we turn to specifics about making major purchases, such as a home or an automobile.

PART 2

MAJOR PURCHASES

6

BUYING AN AUTOMOBILE

New cars cost a lot of money. Even the least expensive, the so called "economy cars," cost approximately $7,000, new. "Moderately-priced" autos go for more than $15,000, and luxury cars cost as much as a house in some areas of the country. Cars have become so expensive, in fact, that with the exception of buying real property, purchasing an automobile is the largest financial transaction that most people ever enter into.

Of course, there's more at stake when you buy a car than money. For example, there is safety. With some 45,000 people killed each year in automobile accidents, safety should definitely be an important factor to consider when buying a car.

This chapter will cover the issues you need to be aware of when buying a car. There is much to consider: how to go about the task of buying a car, how to negotiate the deal, financing and leasing. We will also offer tips on buying a used car and will provide a description of lemon laws designed to protect consumers who get stuck with a car that frequently breaks down.

BUYING A NEW CAR

The following are the most common questions consumers have about buying a new car:

What Is the True Price of Buying a Car?

There are both direct and indirect potential costs involved in buying a car. They include costs that are obvious and others that you may not think about. All should be considered when deciding how much car you can buy for the budget you have to spend:

The List Price. Each new car is sent from the manufacturer to the dealer with what is called a recommended list price. This is the price for the car that will appear on the sticker in the car's window (along with the equipment included with the car and any added equipment that costs extra). With a few exceptions, the list price is designed as an asking price, in reality a starting point for negotiating the actual price that will be paid. (An interesting study reported recently in the *Chicago Tribune* found that some consumers were able to negotiate better deals than others for the same car. White men, not surprisingly, did best and black women did worst. Perhaps that is based on the perception of power in the negotiation but the moral of the story is this: be hard-nosed in your negotiations, be willing to walk out the door and pit different dealerships against each other. In short, make them work for your business.)

The Purchase Price. The purchase price is the price you actually agree to pay for the car. Be sure you find out what features are included in the purchase price, such as air conditioning, cruise control, etc. Often, dealers will give a good purchase price with one hand and take the deal away with the other hand by charging full board on popular extras. Also, pay attention to the equipment that is included in the purchase price, since you may end up paying more for extras.

Additional Options. For an additional price, you can often buy extras that enhance the look, comfort or safety of the car, over the basic model. If you are not careful, the cost of extras, such as that special designer seat fabric package, can raise the cost of the car so much that it is out of the price range you had set for yourself. It is no coincidence that selling options can be a big profit center for auto dealers.

Indirect Costs. There are many indirect costs that also add to the price of a car. You may be charged several taxes when you buy a car, including sales tax (if applicable in your state), and excise taxes. You may also be required to pay a transfer fee (the amount it costs to ship the car from the manufacturer to the sales lot) and the registration fee (to register your car with the Department of Motor Vehicles). Some consumers have successfully negotiated away these two latter charges.

If you trade in an old car for a new car, you may find that the cost of your insurance dramatically increases. This will be especially true if you increase the levels of insurance or take out optional coverage. (For example, many people with older cars do not take out coverage for collision or theft, because it is not worth the premium price. However, if you buy a new car, these options should definitely be obtained, which can increase your total premium by more than one-third.) (For more information on insurance, see Chapter 11.)

Most people borrow money to buy a car, either by obtaining a car loan or through leasing. Yet many don't think of this as increasing the cost of the car since financing is generally sold on the level of monthly payments and not on how much it will add to the price of the car. Yet, financing can add so much to the cost that you could have bought a much better model for cash than the type of car you bought through financing.

In order to keep your warranty in effect, you will have to perform routine maintenance on the car, oil changes, inspections and the like. This must be done by an authorized service outlet, frequently a dealership. Some kinds of cars cost much less than others to do this routine service but may cost more for repairs that are out of warranty. Such expenses are part of the overall price of the car.

The moment you drive your new car off the lot, it loses value, and (unless you own a "classic,") continues to do so for the life of the vehicle. If you buy a car that depreciates a lot, you will lose money when the time comes to trade it in or sell it, thereby adding to the cost of the car.

What Is the Best Way to Shop for a Car?

Shopping for a car can be exciting and fun. It is also an important part of the process since the way you shop will determine the quality of vehicle you purchase and the price. Here is a step-by-step shopping agenda:

Determine How Much You Want to Pay. Buying a new car from a showroom can be as seductive as going into a casino in Las Vegas. Everything is designed to get you to open your wallet and put your money down. That being so, it is important to set limits for yourself before you hit the showrooms. In that way, you won't be "traded up" into a flashy car that costs more than you can really afford.

Research the Cars Available at Your Price. Once you have decided how much you want to pay, research the cars that come within your price range. There are a lot of things to look for in your research.

There may be more cars available in your price range than you think and you don't want to overlook any. Thus, your first step is to get an idea of the range of choices you have. This can be done by looking at newspaper ads or by looking at the annual *Consumer Reports Annual Auto Issue* which is published each spring. The magazine will also offer valuable comparisons of the different models, which can be very helpful.

Safety should be a primary issue, because it directly affects your life and those of your loved ones. Happily, there is a great deal of material published each year on auto safety. There is also a National Highway Traffic Safety Administration New Car Assessment Safety Hotline, which will send you information on crash tests, safety recalls, and the like. The toll free number is (800) 424-9393. *You can also report safety problems to the hotline.* There are other things to look for regarding safety. For example, are safety equipment items, such as a passenger side airbag or anti-lock brakes, standard or optional?

Every new car has a warranty, but some are better than others. The longer and more complete the warranty, the lower the cost of maintenance. The laws regarding car warranties vary from state-to-state. However, all must meet minimum federal standards created by the *Magnuson-Moss Act*. Under the Act, written warranties must disclose the following in clear, understandable language:

- Who is protected? Some warranties only protect first buyers, others are based on time or mileage, not ownership.
- What is protected? Different parts of the vehicle may have different warranties.
- How long is the protection? The time of protection is often measured in time and/or miles.

If you want your transportation to be economical, you will want to explore issues such as gas mileage (it can be found on the sticker), the level of gasoline octane required (the higher the octane the higher the price), the frequency and cost of regular maintenance, etc.

Buying a car is a subjective enterprise. Behind the safety stats, the fuel economy and the price, is the emotional issue of whether a car makes your palms sweat and your heart beat faster. How does it look? How does it drive? Does it have sufficient power to get out of tight spots in a hurry? Is it comfortable? Does it meet your anticipated future needs? The importance of such considerations should not be underestimated and are certainly legitimate. However, they should not predominate over issues such as safety and price.

Get the Best Credit Terms. Most people have to borrow money to buy a new car. Credit unions often offer the best deal to new car buyers. Banks too may provide you good terms. Credit is also available from dealers but only use them as a last resort since they often do not have as beneficial terms.

There is a lot to think about when getting credit to buy a car:

- What is the down payment?
- What are the monthly payments?
- What is the interest rate?
- How long is the loan?
- What is the total price of the loan, including interest and any costs?
- What are the penalties if you get behind in your payments?

These and other issues involving credit will be discussed in more detail in Chapter 13.

Negotiate the Deal. When you go in to the dealer to negotiate the deal, remember, you have the ultimate power in the transaction—you can simply walk out the door. Thus, there is no reason to be rushed into buying. You should also visit more than one dealer to get different sales persons bidding against each other until you get as low a price as you believe you are likely to obtain.

There are other things to keep in mind during the negotiation:

- If you are nervous about such hard-edged business transactions, you may want to bring a friend who is adept at such negotiations to assist you.
- A supervisor may be able to go lower than the salesperson: If you hit a snag, ask to speak with a higher-up. If they really want the sale, they may send in a manager.
- You can often save money by buying a car on the dealer's lot rather than having it ordered from the manufacturer or transferred from another dealer.
- Negotiate the price of a new car before you speak about the value of your trade-in. In that way, you can get a good deal and if you don't like the trade-in offer, you can sell your old car through another method.
- Try to get guaranteed financing in advance. If the salesperson knows you have the borrowing power to buy a car, he or she may work extra hard to get you a good deal so that you will come to a decision then and there.
- Once you negotiate a price, stick to it. A common tactic is for a salesperson to up the price by saying "The manager won't approve this." Don't pay a deposit until the deal is sealed by a manager's signature.

What About Taking Delivery?

Taking delivery is an important part of the purchase, since you may be stuck with what you got once you drive it off the lot.

When taking delivery, be sure and do the following:

- Inspect the car for dents and dings.
- Look at the odometer to see how many miles it has been driven to be sure it is "new."

- Check to make sure the spare tire is in place and that you have a jack.
- Check your invoice and the window sticker to make sure you have received everything you bargained for.

If you discover any problems, get them handled before you leave the lot or get a written agreement from the dealer, identifying the problems that exist and getting the dealer's specific promise to make amends by a certain date.

What About Leasing?

Auto leasing has become a real growth area in the auto industry. When you lease a car, you are renting it for a period of time defined by the lease. Because you are not buying it, you don't have to pay the full price. Thus, your monthly payments for the same car are likely to be much lower than if you paid a small down payment and financed the balance of the purchase price.

Leasing is peddled as a less expensive way to own a more expensive car. But there are drawbacks of which you may not be aware:

You Don't Own the Car. At the end of the lease, you have to turn the car back to the leasing company. There may be a payment owed by you if the actual value of the car is less than the amount that was determined it would be at the end of the lease, at the time the lease was signed. If you choose to buy the car at the end of the lease, there will be a fee charged for the privilege.

You Must Maintain the Car as If It Were Your Own. Most leases compel you to pay for all maintenance and repairs—for a car you will be turning back to the company.

There May Be a Penalty for Excessive Use. Leases typically limit your mileage you can drive per year for the cost of the lease. Exceed that amount, and you pay a penalty at the end of the lease. For example, assume your three-year lease limits you to 15,000 miles per year and charges 15 cents a mile for each mile in excess of 15,000. Assume further that you average 20,000 miles per year. At the end of the lease, you would face a penalty of $2,250 (15 cents x 15,000 miles).

You Can Be Charged for Damage to the Vehicle. If you turn in a vehicle that has suffered the slings and arrows of abundant driving, you may be charged a penalty, if the damage exceeds normal wear and tear. (Be sure to check how the term "wear and tear" is defined in the lease agreement.)

There May Be a Charge for Early Termination. If you choose to terminate a lease early, there may be a penalty assessed.

You May Have an Insurance Gap. Your auto insurance collision and theft policy will only pay the fair market value of the car if it has to be replaced. That may be less than the value of the car established in the lease. This is often called the insurance gap. In the event of such a gap, you are responsible for filling it.

It May Cost More For Insurance. If you lease the car, you will be required by the terms of the lease contract to take out high levels of auto insurance. This level might be more than you would otherwise select, and thus increases the cost of operating the car.

If You Default, You May Have to Pay for the Car. If you get into financial trouble and don't pay on the lease, the car will be repossessed. But that will not be the end of the matter. The leasing company will auction off the car. The amount received at the auction will be deducted from the value of the car as established in the lease, and they can sue you and hold you responsible for the difference, plus any payments you missed. That can make getting out of the financial hole even more difficult than it would otherwise be—plus, you will have virtually paid for a car and have nothing to show for it.

Leasing is a very common method of "buying a car" since it allows people to keep more in their pockets each month than traditional financing. However, there are dangers that can cost you money. Thus, be sure you understand all of the downsides of leasing as well as the benefits before you sign on the dotted line.

BUYING A USED CAR

Used car salesmen have a reputation only a notch above lawyers and politicians. That is because more than one consumer has been taken advantage of in the used car market.

But that doesn't have to happen. Buying a used car can be a good way to get reliable, solid transportation at a reasonable price—if you buy a good used car. Here are some ideas to help you separate the quality pre-owned cars from the worthless klunkers:

Examine the Car Before You Buy. You need to thoroughly examine a used car before you buy it. You should check the odometer, look at the outside for dents and dings, look for rust or any evidence that such damage has been covered up. You should also look under the car for rust or breaks in the frame. It is especially important to look for signs that parts of the frame has been welded together. Check the tires to make sure they match. Also, look at the upholstery. Worn or frayed interiors are a good indication that the car has been heavily used. The same applies to a heavily-worn brake pedal. Look inside the tail pipe. Black, gummy dirt or soot in the tail pipe can mean the car will need extensive repairs.

Take a Test Drive. Pay special attention to how the car handles. Be alert to vibrations. Let the engine idle and listen for noises. How does the car shift gears? Is there smoke coming out of the exhaust? Be on the lookout for sounds, lurches, or other indications that there may be problems. Also, be sure to hit the highway so you can see how the car performs at higher speeds.

Have the Car Inspected. If you are not knowledgeable about cars, you should get your mechanic to inspect the car before you buy it. If the seller refuses, he or she may be hiding something.

Check Out the Reputation of the Vehicle Model. This can be accomplished from several sources:

- *Consumer Reports* has a hotline, (900) 446-1120, that can give you information on frequency of repair, based on model and other such information. As of the date of this writing, the cost is $1.75 per minute.
- Consumer Reports Books publishes a book yearly called *Guide to Used Cars*. It may be in your local bookstore, or you can contact the publisher to purchase it.
- The National Traffic Safety Administration Hotline mentioned above will be able to inform you if the car you are thinking of purchasing has been the subject of a safety recall.

Make Sure You Are Getting a Fair Price. There are many sources that can tell you the fair market value of used cars. One is the *Kelley Blue Book Used Car Guide,* published monthly. The seller probably has a copy. If not, your library will have one as may your auto insurance agent. Another book is the National Automobile Dealers Association's *Official Used Car Guide.* Also, survey your local newspaper's classified ads which should give you a good idea of what the model and year of car you are thinking of buying is selling for in your area. (You may wish to buy from a newspaper ad. If you do, be sure you thoroughly inspect the vehicle, because you are unlikely to be able to achieve satisfaction if you are unhappy with your purchase. Also, make sure the seller actually owned the car, rather than being a used-car salesperson posing as an owner.) *Consumer Reports* rides to the rescue also. They have a used car pricing service hotline that costs $1.75 per minute (as of this writing). It can be reached at (900) 446-1120.

Check Out the Warranty. Used cars may or may not have a warranty. The Federal Trade Commission requires non-private sellers of used cars to display a large sticker in the car window, known as the *Buyer's Guide.* It will tell you if you have a warranty, and if so, what the warranty covers and the time period it is in effect. If the car is sold "As Is," you are on your own, absent fraud. If you buy from a private party, consider the sale, "As Is."

By being careful, you can make a good deal on a used car, whether you buy from a dealer or a private party. But be aware, that buying a used car has risks, among them being that the car may not have the newest safety devices, such as air bags. Thus, take your time, carefully consider your purchase and follow the steps outlined above. Also, try not to buy from a friend. It is a good way to ruin a friendship.

IF YOU BUY A LEMON

If you buy a new car that doesn't operate properly or has chronic problems, you may have bought a poorly constructed car known in the vernacular as a *lemon*. If you have purchased such a citrus fruit when you thought you were buying a reliable form of transportation, take heart. You can obtain satisfaction. Here are some things you can do:

Contact the Dealer

Many people believe that dealers turn a blind eye toward the defects in cars they sell. To quote Ira Gershwin, it ain't necessarily so. Dealers need your business and goodwill to stay in business. This is true even if the warranty has expired, especially if the item was repaired during the warranty period. Remember, dealers want you to refer your friends and return again when it is time to buy your next car. Thus, they are quite likely to take care of the matter in a fair and appropriate fashion. (Be sure to keep copies of your records of complaints and in-warranty service, just in case you are unable to solve your problem at the dealer level.)

Contact the Manufacturer

Every manufacturer will have a regional office to help you with problems. (The address can probably be found in the owner's manual.) If you contact the manufacturer, do so in writing, documenting the efforts you have taken to solve the problems at the dealership level. Manufacturers can often be a big help in resolving problems between you and your dealer.

Arbitrate

If negotiating with the dealer and manufacturer doesn't solve your problem, you can arbitrate. Many manufacturers have arbitration procedures that can be utilized to resolve problems with their vehicles. If you are unable to resolve the dispute through discussions, ask the manufacturer's representative about their programs. The American Automobile Association also offers arbitrations as may local ADR centers.

Sue in Small Claims Court

If the amount involved is less than the jurisdictional amount of your small claims court, going to court is an option for seeking legal redress. (For more details on small claims court, see Chapter 3.)

Invoke Your State's Lemon Laws

If repeated attempts are necessary within the warranty period to repair a repeated defect or problem, and if this defect substantially interferes with your use of the car, or affects its value or safety, you may qualify for relief under your state's lemon laws.

Lemon laws (available in 48 states and the District of Columbia) allow you to return a new car that can't be fixed. You get a full refund or an equivalent replacement vehicle. This does not happen automatically. There are many hoops you have to go through, including:

Making Sure You Qualify. Each state's law will set different requirements to come under lemon law protection: usually four attempts at repairing the same problem, or that the car has been in the shop for 30 days in the first year. To find out the law in your state, contact your state department of consumer affairs.

Notifying the Dealer and Manufacturer That You Are Going to Invoke Your State's Lemon Law. This notification must be in writing (certified mail) and should be done before the car actually qualifies as a lemon (i.e., before taking the car in for the final repair that triggers the lemon law if the repair fails).

Arbitrate. Some lemon laws require you to arbitrate your claim before taking it to court. In most states, the arbitration decision is binding on the manufacturer, not the consumer. Usually, you can continue to drive the car during the arbitration process.

Revoke Your Acceptance. In order to trigger your right to a refund or replacement vehicle, your state's lemon law might require you to revoke your acceptance of delivery of the vehicle (or in other words, relinquishing your car). Revocation must be in writing and must list the specific reasons why you believe you are entitled to return the car. Then, take the car to the dealership, take off the license plates and give the dealer the keys. Do not remove original equipment. Take down the mileage on the odometer.

(Because you are putting your car and perhaps money on the line, you should check with your state's Department of Consumer Affairs or consult with an attorney on the correctness of your case before revoking.)

Prepare to Go to Court. If the dealer does not give you your money back, you may have to sue. Many attorneys specialize in this field. Or, you can go it alone. See Chapter 3 for information on filing a lawsuit. If you win, you may be entitled to more money than the price of the car, as some states permit triple damages for consumers who are successful in bringing lemon-law lawsuits.

Consider Stopping Your Car Payments. Revoking your acceptance may get complicated if you are making payments on the car. If you got your car loan directly, you may be in a pinch, since the bank or credit union is not responsible for the fact that you bought a lemon. Stopping payments could cause you to have a bad credit record or to be sued.

However, if the dealer arranged the financing, you have more power, thanks to a federal regulation known as the *Holder in Due Course Rule*. Under these conditions, your have the same defense against making payments that you would have had against the dealer directly. Be sure to tell the financing company in writing that you consider them "holders in due course" and that you are stopping your car payments unless your car is replaced or a refund is given. In that way, the lender may take action to help you. If they don't, you may not have to pay for your car—but you may have to prove your point in court.

Fighting over lemons can be a time-consuming (some lemon litigations have lasted years) and emotionally draining experience. However, many consumers come out on top. Thus, stand up for your rights. Even if you don't plan to go all the way to litigation, merely letting the manufacturer or dealer know you *know* your legal rights may be enough to obtain a reasonable resolution of the dispute.

For more information on lemon laws, car warranties and tips on dealing with the system, see Appendix 6 (Bibliography).

7

BUYING
A HOME

Buying a home is probably the most exciting, yet most anxiety-producing endeavor most people ever become engaged in. After all, there is much at stake: emotional commitment, quality of life, the fulfillment of the "American Dream," not to mention money—lots and lots of money. That being so, you should approach buying a house with great care and caution.

This chapter will focus on the primary things you need to know when you buy a house. We will touch on the considerations that go into making the choice, discuss how a real estate sale is transacted, and explore such areas as mortgage financing, the added legal obligations of condominium owners, and the terms you should consider if you enter into a real estate purchase.

FINDING THE RIGHT HOME

Finding the "right" home to buy is a purely subjective exercise. The home of my dreams may leave you wanting to find something to ease the queasiness in your stomach and vice-versa. However, there are some standard considerations to think about when looking for that abode you want to make into your home. These include:

Location

For many people location is the most important consideration. Often this is a matter of compromise. For example, property close to work may be too expensive, while a home that comes within a reasonable price range may require a 45-minute commute. If you are judging a locale, consider the following:

- Proximity to work
- Quality of neighborhood, including recreational facilities, schools, safety, etc.
- Nearness of family and friends
- Convenience to the areas you frequent, such as the beach, parks, museums, etc.
- Quality of local infrastructure (roads, sewers)
- Suburb versus urban versus rural, depending on your personal taste

Location will have a primary bearing on the next factor: cost.

Cost

The money you will spend is another big factor in deciding which property to buy. The following should be considered when looking into the issues involving the cost of a house:

Price. The issue of price means more than just the amount to be paid. You want a fair price. Determining a fair price is an inexact science that is determined on several factors.

Formal appraisals: In the home real estate market, most appraisals use a comparison of the house in question with the sales prices received for similar houses in the same neighborhood in recent months.

Comparing the list prices for similar houses: The list price is the seller's asking price. When someone wants to sell property, they usually list it with a real estate agent, who places the property in a computer data bank, usually called the multi-listing service. By comparing the asking price of the house you are interested in with the list prices of similar houses contained in the data-bank (which is available to real estate agents and other subscribers for a price), you can determine whether the asking price seems fair. (This is less exact than obtaining a formal appraisal, since most houses sell for less than their list price. However, comparing list prices can provide enough information for you to make an initial judgment about the price being asked so that you can decide whether to conduct further research.)

The opinion of your real estate agent: Most sellers list their houses with real estate agents. Many buyers also use real estate agents. The seller's agent is known as the listing agent. That agent will make a determination of a good price to list the house for, depending on the needs of the seller. You too, may want to use a real estate agent to help you judge a fair price for the property, since he or she should have a good feel for what property is selling for in the area near the house you are interested in. If you use an agent to help you buy the property, that person is known as the selling agent. (For more on using real estate agents, see below.)

The condition of the property: The better the condition of the premises, generally, the more it is worth. Likewise, a "fixer-upper" or rundown house sold "as is" may offer a substantial bargain.

The condition of the local real estate market: The real estate market is acutely sensitive to the law of supply and demand. Thus, if there are fewer buyers than sellers, a buyer's market is created whereby sellers will often be willing to sell for a lower price in order to get a deal. Conversely, if there are more buyers than sellers, sellers are likely to hang tough on the price and demand full list price. (In a time of buying frenzy, some buyers even buy at higher than list price.)

The "motivation" of the seller: Buying and selling property is an "arms length" transaction. As long as no laws are broken (i.e., no fraud, undo influence, etc.), there are no rules that require you (or entitle you) to pay a "fair price" for the property. Thus, if you know a seller is in financial distress, you can probably offer a lower price than if the seller was in a position to take or leave a purchase offer or has lots of potential buyers from which to choose. Likewise, if the seller knows you are desperate to buy the house, he or she may hold out in order to induce you to pay top-dollar.

Interest Rates: The price of a house is only the most obvious factor in determining the actual cost of the purchase. Another important element is the amount of interest you will have to pay on the mortgage or trust deed you take out in order to make the purchase. Most people are concerned about the monthly payment created as a direct consequence of the rate of interest.

Taxes: Property taxes paid each year add to the cost of a house. On the positive side, property taxes are deductible from your income tax.

Insurance: Ditto for homeowner's insurance, except that insurance is not deductible.

Maintenance and Repair: If you buy a "fixer upper" the cost of repairs and maintenance may add significantly to the cost of the house. Even if the house is in great shape, some homes will cost more to maintain than others. For example, if you get a house with a heated swimming pool, it will cost more to maintain and insure than a similar house without one. The cost of maintenance, repair and utilities will vary from house to house. If that is an issue for you, be sure to ask the seller how much such expenses cost per month.

Mortgage Insurance: If you buy a house and pay less than twenty percent down, you are probably going to have to agree to pay for purchase mortgage insurance (PMI), which insures the institution granting you the home loan. (See below for more details on PMI.)

REAL ESTATE AGENTS

As you can see, deciding what you want in a house and what you can afford can be complicated. For this reason you may want to use a real estate agent to assist you. If you do, here are some considerations to keep in mind:

Agents Can Represent Both Parties

Unlike lawyers who cannot represent more than one party in a business transaction, real estate agents can represent both sides in a real estate purchase contract. However, if you use an agent who also represents the seller, they may not have your best interest at heart since they are trying to get a good price for the house. In fact, the seller's agent has a higher fiduciary obligation to the seller than to the buyer. Thus, many people get their own agent or a lawyer to help them buy, rather than use the seller's agent.

Your "Selling Agent" May Really Represent the Seller

Unless you hire an independent agent and pay for his or her professional services, your real estate agent will be paid a portion of the commission earned by the listing agent. (Real estate agents typically receive five to six percent of the selling price as a commission, which is usually split equally between the listing and selling agents.) Since your agent is, in reality, being paid by the seller, he or she may be considered a sub-agent of the listing agent, unless your state law states otherwise. Thus, before revealing important data to your agent that you would not want the seller to know, ask your agent to disclose who he or she owes his or her highest duty of loyalty to: you, or the seller.

A Real Estate Agent Can Be a Big Help

The above notwithstanding, a real estate agent can offer you a wide variety of services that can help you in your real estate purchase:

They Can Shorten Your Search. Your agent should be able to show you to the houses which meet your needs, such as size, price, amenities, etc. By pointing you in the right direction, your search can be considerably shortened.

They Can Tell You How Much Home You Can Afford. Real estate agents know a lot about mortgage financing, down payments and most other financial aspects of buying a house. They can tell you approximately the size of loan you can qualify for, the different types of mortgages that may be available, the monthly payments you could expect to pay depending on the type of loan you obtain and about other costs associated with the purchase.

They Can Make Sure Important Clauses Are Placed in the Contract. There are a lot of tricks to the trade of buying a house and your real estate agent should use his or her professional training and experience for your benefit. This should specifically include contract clauses that protect your interests, such as contingency clauses, including fixtures as part of the sale, and so forth.

They Do the Negotiating. Negotiations can be difficult, tension-ridden interactions. For example, you may want to make an offer far below the asking price. Doing it through your agent may be easier than doing it face-to-face. Or, if you passionately want the property, you may want a "cool head" in the negotiations, to keep you from "giving away the store."

They Can Tell You What Will Happen. Buying a house is a complex, sometimes frustrating transaction where legalities must be strictly adhered to. Understanding the procedure and what will be happening step-by-step can go a long way toward reducing tension and anxiety. Your real estate agent can also monitor the transaction as it progresses from agreement to completed contract so that you will always know what is going on.

They Are Responsible to Do a Professional Job. If you use a real estate agent to represent you and you get stuck in a bad situation because of a deficiency in the contract, you can hold your agent responsible, if the deficiency was caused by your agent's negligence or misconduct.

Real Estate Agents and Ethics

Real estate agents must meet ethical standards established by the state. If they do not, they can lose their license, in much the same manner that a lawyer or doctor can lose their licenses. (Which in the real world means that few ever do.) If you have questions about the ethical obligations of your agent, contact the local real estate board. You can also contact the National Association of Realtors® and ask for a copy of their published code of ethics. (The NAR is the largest trade association in the real estate industry. Among its purposes is public education and the promulgation of ethics in the real estate business. Only real estate agents who belong to a local board affiliated with the national association can call themselves a "realtor®.")

MAKING THE PURCHASE

Buying a home should be approached with caution, deliberation and a sense of seriousness. This is a very big deal. How you negotiate the sale will have a material impact on your future—and your finances.

Okay. Assume you have found your dream house. It's perfect: The right size, in the right location, with a look and feel that you've dreamed of living in your whole life. Now, the time has come to negotiate the purchase. Here are some tips:

Ask For Written Disclosures of Defects

Like a book, you cannot judge a house by its cover. Or to quote another cliché that is true for all of its familiarity, appearances can be deceiving. Thus, before you make an offer, ask the seller or the seller's agent (or have your agent ask) for a full, written disclosure of all known defects or problems associated with the property, or other facts that could be material to your decision. (Some states require such disclosure by law. Others do not.)

Make an Offer

The negotiation will begin with your *offer*. An offer can be described as a request to enter into a contract under the terms specified in the offer. (The offer should be in writing.) If the offer is accepted, its terms become the basis for the contract. This being so, you should be very careful about what you offer. Here are some things to think about:

The Price. You will probably want to make an offer beneath the listing price (the price at which the house is offered) but not so low as not to be taken seriously (unless you are trolling for a very good deal and do not want to pay a price close to market value).

The Date the Transaction Is to Be Completed. In order to ensure that the matter moves forward promptly, a date by which the transaction is to be completed (sometimes called the closing date) should be included in the offer.

Who Pays the Costs of Sale. Every real estate deal has costs involved and the contract should specify which party is responsible. These costs include: the appraisal fee, the transfer fee, credit report fee, title search, title insurance, notary fee, transfer tax, recording fees, etc. The offer should specify who pays what cost.

The Amount of "Earnest Money." Your written offer should state that you are prepared to back up your offer with a cash deposit—called "earnest money," usually an amount between $1,000 and $5,000. Earnest money shows the seller you are serious and binds the deal as a form of consideration. (It is not the down payment required by a lender but can be part of the down payment.) You should also make clear whether your earnest money is refundable if the deal falls apart in your offer.

Contingency Clauses. It is very important for your offer to include contingency clauses that will let you cancel the real estate contract under specific conditions. For example, you should always make the contract contingent upon obtaining financing so that the seller can't sue in the event the deal is not completed because of your inability to obtain a loan. You should also make the deal contingent upon your having the house inspected and your approving the condition of the property. The contract should also be contingent upon the seller having clear *title.* (The official record of ownership.) There are other contingency clauses you may wish to include in your offer. For more details, ask your agent or attorney.

What Is to Be Included in the Sale. A controversy can often arise between a buyer and a seller as to exactly what goes with the house in the sale. For example, unless you specify, removable items, such as the refrigerator, will not be included in the purchase price. On the other hand, fixtures, items permanently attached to the property, such as a built-in stove, will be included unless otherwise specified. Pay particular attention to this detail. For example, if you love those walnut bookcases in the living room, or the chandelier in the dining room, specifically list them as being part of the sale.

Rent Prohibition. Until title officially passes to you, the seller is legally able to rent the property to others. This could create a real headache. Thus, always put a clause in the contract prohibiting the seller from renting the property while the sale of the house in pending.

Termite Inspection. You will want to have the property inspected for termite infestation and/or damage. If such problems are discovered, be sure the seller is responsible for all repairs.

Note: There are real estate forms available for making offers that embody many of the above terms. They can be obtained in legal stationery stores and can be used. However, feel free to modify the terms on the form if you choose.

Review the Counter Offer

With very rare exceptions, your initial offer will not be accepted in full. Rather, it will either be rejected (at which point, the transaction is over) or there will be a counter offer.

Legally, a counter offer is a rejection of your original offer with a new offer then being made to you. A counter offer will often accept some of the terms from the original offer and request changes in others, or add new terms. For example, an offer to buy a house for $100,000 might be "countered" at $110,000, while accepting all other terms of the original offer. Thus, in this example, the terms of the counter offer will be identical to the first offer, except for the difference in price.

Once you receive the counter offer, you can:

Reject It. At this point the transaction is completed and no one owes the other any obligation.

Accept It. If you accept the counter offer, its terms will be the basis of the purchase contract, including terms from your original offer that were not changed in the counter offer.

Counter the Counter Offer. You can counter the counter offer, which has the same effect as that already stated. Negotiations will continue in that manner, often with many counter offers flying back and forth between the parties until a deal is struck or negotiations are terminated.

Note: Be sure to keep all of this paperwork because you may have to reconstruct the negotiation of the contract if there is ever a dispute as to the terms that had been agreed upon.

The Final Contract of Sale

After the last counter offer is finally accepted, the document will be signed by both parties and the contract will have been entered into. At that point, both parties are obligated to perform according to its terms.

Most offers and counter offers in real estate deals are made in writing. However, if you made an oral deal, be aware that the contract itself *must* be reduced to writing. The reason for this is the *Statute of Frauds.* Under the Statute of Frauds, if your deal is not in writing, the court will not enforce it, except under very limited circumstances. (For example, if you paid the full price of the deal to the land owner, who then absconded with it and refused to transfer title.)

If you have questions about the contract, be sure to ask them of the other side before signing. You should also get any understandings as to the meaning of terms in writing, either in the contract itself or by confirming letter. If you are represented by a real estate agent, be sure to ask the agent to review the agreement. If you have a lawyer representing you, you should have him or her explain it.

Getting Financing

Few people can afford to pay cash when they buy a house, and many who can will decide to finance because interest paid on a home purchase mortgage is deducted against income tax. Thus, most home purchases are made with mortgage or trust deed financing. The following are some of the most important things to know about mortgage financing:

Types of Mortgages. Mortgages come in two basic types: fixed rate and variable rate. A fixed-rate mortgage keeps the same interest rate for the life of the loan; typically, 30 years. This also means the monthly payment remains unchanged for the life of the mortgage.

A variable-rate mortgage starts at a lower interest rate than a fixed-rate mortgage. However, the interest charged on the loan will vary every year, based on a formula contained in the contract that ties your interest to the fluctuations of an identified major economic index. This means that the mortgage payment will rise and fall, depending on economic conditions. Thus, if you apply for a variable-rate mortgage (which will have an initial interest lower than a fixed-rate mortgage), be sure there is a cap in the agreement above which the interest rate cannot go, otherwise it is a risky deal. Also be sure to limit the amount that the interest can rise each year so as to prevent sudden large increases in your monthly mortgage payments. It is usually easier to qualify for a variable-rate mortgage; however, over the life of the loan, a variable-rate mortgage is likely to be more expensive.

The Down Payment. In order to get a loan, the mortgage lender will usually require you to put money down, typically twenty percent. With the price of real estate being what it is in many locales, this can be a problem, especially for first-time buyers, since a $300,000 property would require $60,000 down (plus closing costs).

Some lenders will permit a lower down payment, even as low as five percent, if you obtain purchase mortgage insurance (PMI). The premiums for the PMI will be based on a percentage of the mortgage amount, typically one-half to one percent up-front and the same amount each year thereafter, paid in equal monthly installments. PMI companies are very picky about the property they insure. As a result, many deals fall through when PMI carriers refuse to issue a policy because of a defect in the property or because they do not agree with the lender's appraisal of the value of the property.

Points. Most mortgage lenders charge an up-front fee for making the loan, euphemistically called "points." One point equals one percent of the loan. Thus, a $100,000 mortgage financed at two points, would cost $2,000, in addition to interest charges. (The points are usually paid through the loan; in the example above, the loan would actually fund at $102,000.)

Foreclosure. If the borrower defaults on the loan, the mortgage holder has the right to foreclose on the property; that is, have the property seized and sold at public auction to pay the unpaid balance on the loan.

Usually foreclosure is the lender's only remedy if the loan goes into default. However, if the loan is not a purchase money mortgage (for example, if it is a refinancing loan to pay off debts), the lender may be able to foreclose and sue you for any unpaid balance. Before taking out a nonpurchase money mortgage (including an equity loan or equity-backed credit card which used to be called a second mortgage), be sure to ask about the lender's remedies in the event of a default.

Closing the Deal

After you and the seller have performed all of your obligations under the contract, such as obtaining financing and signing transfer papers, the deal will be concluded. Depending on where you live, this is known as the *closing, title closing, settlement* or *escrow.*

Often the closing takes place at a meeting of all those involved. When that happens, the process is commonly called a settlement. If no meeting occurs, it's more often known as escrow and is handled by an escrow agent. In such cases, you and the seller usually sign an agreement to deposit certain funds and documents with the escrow company, which acts as an agent for both sides. When all the papers and funds are in, the escrow is closed and the agent records the documents and makes the appropriate payments.

Note: Escrow instructions can be used to modify contracts and will often be deemed by the court as setting forth the terms of the contract itself. Thus, be sure and review these documents carefully to ensure their accuracy.)

Settlement involves much more than the formal acts of passing the papers. All the details, loose ends and additional services required to conclude the deal must be tended to. This is when the full cost of buying a home becomes clear—not just the purchase price or the cost of the loan to buy it, but the actual cost of the process of buying as well. Be warned: these closing costs can add up to eight percent of the purchase price of the home! As the buyer, you can expect to pay three to six percent of this purchase price sum in closing costs.

The Obligations of Property Owners

Property owners have obligations to their community and neighborhood that can be enforced in a court of law. Briefly, these obligations include:

Paying Property Taxes. Property taxes must be paid, or the taxing municipality can seize the property and sell it at auction to pay for the back taxes and penalties. The amount of property tax is usually based on a percentage of the appraised value of the property.

Meeting Local Codes. If a homeowner wants to improve the property, he or she will have to comply with local building codes. The use of the property (e.g. residential, commercial, etc.) will be limited by local zoning regulations.

Maintaining the Property. Municipalities can use civil and criminal laws to prevent property owners from permitting their property from falling into disrepair and then becoming a public hazard. Failure to maintain the property can also result in a civil suit brought against the owner by neighbors.

Complying with Home Owners' Association Rules. Some neighborhoods have home owners' associations, which set rules on the upkeep of the homes under their jurisdictions. Home owners' associations can set standards of upkeep, paint color, home improvements, building heights and other such matters that would normally be exclusively under the property owner's control. Home owners' association rules can often be enforced in court.

Condominium Ownership

In addition to the above, owners of condominiums and town homes have special rules that apply:

Each Owner Owns His or Her Own Unit and a Proportionate Share of the Common Areas. If you own a condo, you must pay the expenses of maintaining your own unit and pay your share of maintaining common areas such as lawns, walkways, swimming pools, roofs, and the like. These payments are made through dues to the Condominium Association.

Each Owner Must Join the Condominium Association. All management decisions for the condominium complex will be made by the condominium association, usually through its board of directors, a small group of owners elected by the association members. Usually, the directors will hire professional managers to handle the day-to-day management activities.

Each Owner Must Pay Association Dues. To make sure that the complex is maintained, each owner pays dues to the association. The dues pay for maintenance, normal repairs, insurance, the complex manager's salary and other such expenses. The amount of the dues will be established by the board, usually in an amount sufficient to pay for normal maintenance and repairs and to create a surplus fund in case of emergency. Failure to pay dues can result in a lawsuit and or *lien* (a legal claim) being placed on the owner's condominium property.

The Association Can Levy a Special Assessment. In an emergency, a special assessment can be charged by the association to improve or repair the complex. For example, if there is a mud slide that damages the property, the owners can be assessed the money it will take to repair the damage, even if an owner's individual unit was undamaged. The amount of the special assessment will be paid by the owners in the same proportion as their usual dues.

The Association Sets the Rules For the Complex. The condominium association sets rules that all residents of the condominium complex must obey, be they owners or renters. These rules may range from prohibiting owners from parking their cars in their driveways, to requiring association permission before improving a unit, to a prohibition against playing a stereo too loudly. Failure to obey the rules can result in fines being assessed by the association or other enforcement actions.

If you own a condominium it is very important that you participate in your association's decision-making process, since you will be bound by the decisions of the group and its board of directors.

PART 3

OBTAINING SERVICES

8

GETTING YOUR
AUTO REPAIRED

Approximately four out of five American households own one or more automobiles. If there is one thing that can be said with certainty about all of these cars it is that they will need maintenance and repair. That puts many at a disadvantage because most people know as much about auto repair as they do about brain surgery. This lack of knowledge leaves many of us vulnerable to rip-offs.

According to a recent U.S. Department of Transportation study, about forty percent of the costs associated with auto repairs are unnecessary. That comes to about $40 billion a year. The following are the primary problems associated with auto repair as identified by the government:

- Unneeded parts sold in package deals
- Unneeded repairs due to poor diagnosis
- Faulty repairs for which the car's owner did not get his or her money back
- Unneeded repairs sold with fraudulent intent
- Accidents due to faulty repairs

In fact, auto repair fraud has gotten so bad, the insurance industry has organized to combat it, with mixed results.

Auto repair problems can be a major legal headache, and in many locales are the most complained-about consumer problem. One reason for this is that a lot of people don't know the difference between an odometer and a carburetor. That leaves many at the mercy of the honesty of the mechanic. Also, when you take a car to a garage for repair, the mechanic can keep possession of the car until full payment for the repairs is made. (This is called a *mechanic's lien.*) Then, there is the problem of paying for a repair, finding that the car was not fixed correctly, yet having a mechanic who refuses to finish the job without extra cost. For this reason, many state and local consumer affairs offices have passed special rules that apply to auto repair.

For example, more than half the states and the District of Columbia have "truth in auto repair" or "good-faith disclosure" laws. Such laws require repair shops to give consumers written estimates, to notify them in advance if the estimate will be exceeded, to return replaced parts, and to itemize repair bills, stating whether the parts installed were used, new, or repaired.

Disclosure laws vary. In Maryland, written estimates are required only on repairs that exceed $50, and a customer can be charged up to ten percent more than the estimate without being contacted in advance. In California, however, customers must get written estimates on *all* repairs before any work is done, and they cannot be charged more than the estimate unless they have approved the charge in advance.

The best way to protect yourself is to know what the laws are in your state. For more information, call your local or state Office of Consumer Affairs. Most of these offices offer basic advice and distribute pamphlets that describe your state's laws regulating auto repairs.

This chapter points the way toward finding a good mechanic, discusses how to approach car repairs with confidence and informs you of your options if you are unhappy with the quality of the service you receive.

HOW TO APPROACH AUTO REPAIRS

Since prevention is the best way to legally protect your interests, making sure you get the proper repairs at a fair price takes a plan of action on your part. Here's a good approach:

Find the Right Repair Facility For Your Car's Problem

It is important to match your car's problems with the proper repair facility to fix it. There are several kinds of repair service facilities available. Many gas stations also service cars. So do all new-car dealerships. In addition, some department stores such as Sears and Montgomery Ward offer auto repair services. Then there are the national chains that offer specialized repairs for items like mufflers, brakes and transmissions, and entrepreneurs who work as independent mechanics.

Some of these facilities may be good for some types of repairs but not others. For example, if you are going to have basic maintenance performed, such as an oil change, or are buying new tires, a department store auto-repair facility may provide good service and parts and a less expensive price than an entrepreneur or dealership. On the other hand, if the repair is going to be complex and expensive, the dealer or qualified garage may be better than the department store. If you need specialized service, such as a new muffler or brake job, a national chain may be your best bet. If you don't know what is wrong, you may want to go to your usual mechanic or a garage that can give you a diagnosis.

Finding the right repair facility or mechanic begins with an organized approach, whether it is finding someone to handle your car's usual maintenance (oil change, filter change, etc.) or to diagnose and repair specific problems. (A trustworthy repair facility is one that performs only those repairs that are really required, does so in a timely manner and at a price that is fair.) Finding that pot of gold at the end of the rainbow takes time and effort on your part. Here are some tips:

Get Referrals From Friends. Ask your friends and loved ones who live near you if they are happy with their mechanic or garage. If they are, ask why. If you trust their judgment and if their car is similar to yours, you may wish to check out their mechanic.

Find Out If the Mechanics Are Certified. Mechanics can be voluntarily certified by the *National Institute for Automotive Service Excellence (NIASE)*. There are 24 total certifications issued by the Institute, eight in the field of auto repair. Some certifications are given in specific areas of auto repair. Thus, a mechanic certified in steering may not know enough about automatic transmission. However, a "Master Automobile Technician" is certified in all NIASE areas of auto repair certification. Look for the Blue Seal of Excellence in front of the facility. That means there should be certified technicians within. (However, for the ambitious consumer, NIASE also recommends that you ask to see the technician certification papers before going forward.)

Note: Certification does not mean that the mechanic will do a good job. But it does mean that the mechanic cared enough about his or her profession to take the time to study and was sufficiently proficient to pass the skills tests required for certification.

Check With the AAA. The Automobile Association of America (AAA) also approves repair facilities in many states, based on a review of equipment, mechanic qualifications and customer satisfaction. By going to an AAA-approved facility, you will have their seal of approval to rely on, and, perhaps more importantly, you will have someone to complain to (or threaten to complain to) if you are not treated well. Since the mechanic will not be anxious to lose the AAA seal of approval, he or she may be more apt to do right by you rather than risk your making a fuss at the AAA. The AAA's nearest office will be listed in your telephone book.

Check With the BBB. The Better Business Bureau (BBB) may have a record of complaints against the repair facility you are interested in. And if you are unhappy, you can threaten to go to the BBB, thereby letting the garage know they may lose the future business of people who check with the BBB when looking for a mechanic. If the mechanic still refuses to accommodate you, file a complaint with the BBB. The BBB chapter in your locale can be found in your telephone book.

Look For Authorized Repair Shops. Many manufacturers authorize repair facilities to service their vehicles. While authorized repair facilities do not guarantee quality, they at least indicate that the mechanics inside should have experience working on the kind of car you drive. Plus, if you receive poor service, you can complain to the manufacturer, which might withdraw the authorization if too many customers leave the facility unhappy.

Dealing With the Mechanic

Once you find a mechanic you like, you should approach the repair in an organized way:

Write Down the Problems with Your Car. Writing down the problems you have with your car ahead of time will aid you in making sure all of the work is performed that needs to be done.

Go to a Diagnostic Clinic. Some people worry that their mechanic will tell them that more is wrong than actually is. For that reason, you may wish to take your car to a diagnostic clinic. They can tell you what is wrong with the car without the potential conflict of interest of also being the facility that will be doing the actual repairs. You can then take their report to the mechanic who will actually repair the car.

Ask For a Written Estimate. Always get a written estimate of what the repair is going to cost. (In most states, the mechanic must legally give you one.) Also, write the following words on the work order before signing it: *"If my car requires any additional parts and labor over the estimate, contact me for authorization before performing any work not already authorized by me."* That should go a long way toward not making you a victim of an unauthorized repair scam because you do not have to pay for work you do not authorize.

Get a Second Opinion. If you receive an estimate that is in the stratosphere, you may want to get a second opinion from another facility before committing to the repair.

Ask If the Work Is Guaranteed. Different repair facilities differ as to whether they give warranties for work. (One advantage of a national chain or franchise is that they generally give warranties which will be honored by other chain shops.) When discussing the warranty, ask about the length of the warranty (usually measured in time or miles) and the extent of the warranty. For example, does the warranty include both parts and labor?

Inspect All Used Parts. Tell the garage you will want to see all of the replaced parts. In that way they are less likely to take out a perfectly fine water pump when all you needed was a new thermostat.

If You Are Unhappy with the Service

If you are unhappy with the service you have received, there are several tactics you can use to enforce your rights:

Complain to the Service Manager. Your first step is to go to the garage's service manager if you are unhappy. Gather together your paperwork, and be prepared to otherwise prove that the problem you sought to have fixed, isn't. That may include taking the service manager for a ride in the car to prove your point.

Go Up the Ladder. If talking with the service manager does not do the trick, go to the owner of the garage, a general manager, or whomever has ultimate authority. Send that person a letter of complaint, and follow up with a telephone call to make sure the letter was received and is being acted upon. Be sure and let them know what a loyal customer you are and how you would hate to have to tell your friends that the shop cannot be trusted. Also tell the person in authority that if he or she will not give you satisfaction, you will complain to others who may be more persuasive. (See below.) If necessary, make an appointment to see the person in the flesh.

Take the Car to Another Mechanic. To make sure that your car has not been properly repaired, spend the money to have it independently analyzed. This should cost less than $100. Get a written statement from the independent mechanic as to what is wrong with your car and then go back to the repair shop and ask that the problem be fixed for free if the problem involves their improper repair. (If your car is under warranty, do not allow the independent mechanic to repair the car, because it could void your warranty.) If the shop still refuses to give you satisfaction, this statement can be used as evidence to support your position.

Call in the Cavalry. If you are still unhappy, it is time to say, no more Mr. or Ms. Nice Guy, and complain to the powers that be.

Contact the manufacturer: If the dealership is authorized, go to the manufacturer, express your displeasure, prove you are right with as much documentation as possible and ask them to intervene.

Contact the CBBB's AUTO LINE: This is a national program established by the Council of Better Business Bureaus (CBBB) to settle disputes between consumers and certain automobile manufacturers who have agreed to arbitrate complaints when mediation fails. General Motors, American Motors and a dozen foreign car manufacturers have all contracted with the CBBB to offer arbitration to their new-car owners. For more information, call the CBBB at (703) 276-0100.

Contact AUTOCAP: AUTOCAP stands for Automotive Consumer Action Panel. It was established by the National Automobile Dealers Association to resolve disputes informally between new-car/truck dealers and their customers. When you file a dispute with AUTOCAP, it is sent to the dealer, who is given a chance to settle directly with you. If any agreements are made during this time, the dealer is obligated to notify AUTOCAP. You can reach AUTOCAP at (703) 821-7000.

Contact a Consumer Protection Agency: Actions taken by state workers on your behalf can be quite effective. (Although the effectiveness of individual state consumer protection agencies vary.) Whether the consumer affairs people will come to your aid depends on how egregious your problem is and whether the agency has the money in its budget to pursue your complaint. (Many consumer agencies have more complaints than they have the budget to process.) If your complaint seems to be on the back burner, write a follow-up letter asking for information about the progress of the agency's investigation. When you receive notice in the mail that your complaint is being looked into, write down the name and telephone number of the person doing the investigating. You might want to call and ask what will be happening step-by-step. Also, if things bog down, don't be afraid to give them a call to "stimulate" their interest in your case.

But don't stop there. Your state's Department of Transportation or Department of Motor Vehicles may be in charge of licensing garages and your complaint to them may carry clout. Also, if fraud or the violation of other laws was involved, contact your state office of the Attorney General.

Pursue Your Rights in Small Claims Court. If the case comes under the monetary jurisdiction of the small claims court, go for it. You may want to bring in the independent mechanic who analyzed the problems as a witness. Also, you'll want to provide invoices and proof of additional expenses you have incurred because of the faulty work.

Pursue Your Rights Under Lemon Laws. This only applies to new cars. (See Chapter 6.)

Contact Your Credit Card Company. Using a credit card to pay for repairs can give you extra clout, since if you are unhappy with the service you received, you can ask the credit card company not to pay the repair facility for the repair. Then, follow the procedures for dealing with such complaints provided in the law. (See Chapter 13 for details.) The fact that the garage may not get paid for the work can provide a powerful incentive for them to finish the job they started and this time get it right.

There are more state and local laws protecting consumers in auto repair situations than you can shake a crank shaft at. That means you have rights that can be enforced and procedures in place to permit you to do so.

You can usually resolve auto repair problems without legal assistance. However, if you decide to consult an attorney with your auto repair problem, the Center for Auto Safety has compiled a list of lawyers who specialize in auto repair problems. Send a self-addressed stamped envelope to:

Center for Auto Safety
Attn: Lemon Lawyers
2001 S Street, NW
Washington D.C. 20009
(202) 328-7700

9

RETAINING
A LAWYER

In this increasingly complex and legalistic society, knowing how to hire a lawyer is an important consumer-protection skill. Whether you want to hire a lawyer to sue someone, to help you with a real estate transaction, or to resolve a dispute with a car manufacturer, or for any other reason, your chances of receiving quality representation depends on your ability to find the right lawyer and understand the workings of the relationship.

This chapter will cover many of the most important issues that face clients when retaining a lawyer. We will describe how to hire a lawyer, how lawyers get paid, and what to do if you are unhappy with your lawyer. We will also discuss retainer agreements and give you some helpful tips on doing your part as a client to make the relationship work.

DECIDE IF YOU NEED A LAWYER

Not every legal problem requires hiring a lawyer. In fact, many of the issues written about in this book do not require you to hire a lawyer. Here is a list of some of the areas where, in most cases, you can take care of your own problem:

- A situation capable of being handled in small claims court (see Chapter 3)
- Purchasing or selling a house (unless required for title search and the like)
- Purchasing a car and handling warranty problems (however, if you pursue your rights under lemon laws, seriously consider at least conferring with a lawyer)
- Writing a simple will or trust
- Handling a simple divorce (a short marriage with no children and little property)
- Handling a simple auto accident case
- Handling most insurance matters
- Complaining about shoddy or defective products
- Filing for a simple, personal bankruptcy (See Chapter 14)
- Creating a power of attorney
- Changing your name
- Incorporating a business
- Traffic court, unless the violation involves driving while intoxicated
- A simple probate case (unless required by your state's law)
- Step-parent adoption

Here are some examples when you should seriously consider retaining a lawyer to assist you:

- If the case involves a lot of money, significant civil rights or if the case will be complex
- Writing a living trust that requires tax planning
- A contested divorce with child custody, significant property issues or a marriage of long duration where alimony or the right to retirement benefits might be at stake
- A legal malpractice claim
- A will contest
- A prenuptial agreement (for second and subsequent marriages where money, property and children may be an issue)
- A case involving serious physical injury (personal injury, medical malpractice, etc.)
- A case involving fraud
- A case against a large corporation or insurance company,

if it involves significant sums
- A criminal case, other than in traffic court
- Business ownership matters

HOW TO HIRE A LAWYER

If you decide you want a lawyer to assist you with your problem, you will want someone who will be ethical, competent and reasonably priced. (Yes, such lawyers do exist.) Your first job as a client is to find one.

That may be easier said than done. There are a lot of lawyers out there, and telling the good lawyers from those who would take advantage of you or who are not competent will take time and effort on your part. However, finding the right lawyer is the best thing you can do to make sure your significant legal problem is handled in an appropriate and efficient manner. Here's a step-by-step guide for finding good legal help:

Step 1: Identify Your Problem

Lawyers, like doctors, specialize in certain areas of practice. Thus, a lawyer who practices eighty percent in divorce law and twenty percent in real estate may not know much more than he or she learned in law school about, say, securities transactions, and he or she will have forgotten most of that. That being so, your first step is to identify the kind of problem you have. Thus, if you are getting a divorce, you need a divorce lawyer, not one who works as a corporate lawyer. If you want to sue over an auto accident, you want a personal injury attorney, etc.

Step 2: Compile a List of Lawyers You Want to Interview

Once you have identified your problem, you need to find the names of lawyers who practice in your area of need. How do you do that? Here are some suggestions:

Ask People You Know. Referrals from satisfied clients is the way most lawyers build their businesses. Therefore, if your friend had a divorce and liked her lawyer and you too are getting a divorce, you may want to consider your friend's lawyer. However, if your friend liked his securities lawyer and you want to contest a will, that lawyer may not be for you.

Ask Groups Related to Your Legal Concern. You can also get names of attorneys from groups that work on issues related to your legal concern. These may be private organizations, government agencies, or public interest groups such as HALT.

Law Schools and Legal Clinics. Law schools and private legal clinics are other sources of lawyer prospects. Many law schools operate legal clinics to give their students "real world" experience on legal cases under the supervision of attorneys. Most of these clinics serve clients with limited incomes and charge no fees and are generally very helpful on issues such as employment discrimination, landlord/tenant disputes or bankruptcy. However, some law school clinics specialize by subject area, such as small-business law, and serve clients regardless of income.

Check the Yellow Pages and Local Newspapers. More and more lawyers advertise their areas of expertise, and in some cases fee requirements, in the Yellow Pages and local newspapers. While word-of-mouth referrals tend to be more reliable, you shouldn't overlook this option as a possible referral source.

Contact Bar Association Referral Services. Most state and local bar associations have lawyer referral services run for the benefit of their members. However, you can use these services (usually at no or nominal cost) to direct you to lawyers who practice in your area of need. But, it is important to realize that just because a bar association refers a lawyer, that does not mean the lawyer is "good." For the most part, an association refers based on a lawyer putting his or her name on a list. When their turn comes up, the referral is made. In other words, a bar referral does not imply that the lawyer has been screened for competence.

Referral From an Insurance Company. If you are sued for an auto accident or on your homeowners insurance, your insurance company will provide your defense and choose the lawyer. (Generally, you won't want to hire your own lawyer in such cases, unless you may be liable for moneys above what the insurance company will pay or you want to cross complain against the person suing you.)

Prepaid Legal Service Plan. If you are a member of a prepaid legal service plan, the plan may refer you to lawyers on its list of approved lawyer plan participants.

Look in Books. Some books list lawyers in each state and give their areas of specialization. The most notable is the *Martindale-Hubble Law Directory*, which not only lists lawyers but gives their biographies, date of admittance and also rates them on legal competence and ethics, as well. (The ratings are based on the opinions of other lawyers and judges, which may or may not be accurate.) Also note that the lack of a rating does not mean the lawyer is a bad lawyer. Another lawyer directory to check out is the *Law and Business Directory of Litigation Attorneys* by Prentice Hall.

Ask Other Lawyers. Lawyers usually know which of their colleagues are "good" and which are not. Thus, if you know and respect a lawyer who does not practice in your area of concern, (or who does but whom you are not going to hire because, for example, he or she is a friend), ask the lawyer for a referral. They can usually steer you away from the bad apples.

Step 3: Research the Lawyers on Your List

Once you have several names, you should do some research. Much of this can be done over the telephone, by talking to your referral sources or by looking in books in the law library. Look for answers to the following questions:

- What was it, in particular, that induced the referral source to suggest a particular lawyer?
- Was the referral based on a belief in the lawyer's competence? If so, how was that determination made?
- Was there a referral fee involved?
- How many years has the lawyer practiced in my area of concern?
- How many years has the lawyer practiced? (A newer

lawyer will probably cost less. However, a more experienced lawyer will probably be better if your problem is complex.)

- Does the lawyer give free or low-cost initial interviews?

You should also contact your state bar association to see if the lawyer has been publicly disciplined for unethical conduct. (See below.) You can also ask the lawyer for a referral to satisfied clients. However, the names of clients are privileged information under the law and the lawyer cannot give a name without the client's consent.

Step 4: Interview Your Top Prospects

Once you have reduced your list to two or three names, you will want to interview them all for the job. (Remember, you are the one hiring the lawyer. He or she *needs* you, you don't need that particular lawyer—there are many others out there who could serve you well. So there is no reason to be shy or intimidated.) It is important to take the time to do this because the more thorough you are in finding the right lawyer, the more likely it will be that you won't have troubles later on.

When interviewing the lawyer, be ready to tell him or her about your legal problem. If the matter is somewhat complicated, you may want to write the lawyer a letter explaining the matter ahead of time. In that way the lawyer will be up-to-speed on your case, which saves time, and you are less likely to leave anything out. You should also listen. This is your chance to get to know the lawyer, to see if you are comfortable with him or her, and see if the communication between you works well.

You should ask the lawyer his or her opinion about your case. If it is a litigation, you might ask what your chances are of winning. If you want to engage in negotiations with another party, the lawyer may want to tell you the options you have to accomplish your stated goals. You should write this down to compare what each of the other lawyers on your list says to you.

There are also several questions you should ask:

What Do You Charge? The cost of the lawyer may be a primary concern for you. To reduce the chance of future billing disputes, have your lawyer commit his or her fee requirements to writing, including how you will be charged: By the hour? A contingency fee? A flat fee?

What Is Your Best Estimate of What the Case Will Cost and How It Will Be Charged? In your written fee agreement, your lawyer should be able to give you a general ball park figure of the costs of the case, including, if it involves litigation, a worst case scenario on "out-of-pocket" expenses. Expenses can include, among other things, the cost of telephone calls, postage, photo-copying and travel.

Have You Handled This Kind of Case Before? This is your chance to get the lawyer to prove to you that his or her experience suits your needs.

Do You Carry Malpractice Insurance? Even good lawyers can make a mistake. Malpractice insurance is there to protect you, as well as the lawyer, from the financial consequences of your lawyer's mistakes. You may want to ask for proof of coverage, since, according to some estimates, as many as fifty percent of lawyers "go bare" (they don't carry insurance).

What Specific Actions Do You Recommend? Don't accept generalities. You need specifics, so you can decide how to proceed, and so you can compare what different lawyers you interview are saying about your legal problem. If all agree, you can be pretty sure the recommendations are worthwhile. If there is significant disagreement, you may need to discuss the matter further.

What Will Be Happening, Step-By-Step? This question is important because it will give you an idea as to what will occur if you elect to proceed.

What Problems Do You Anticipate? You need to know the bad news as well as the good in order to make informed decisions about your case.

Do You Continue Your Legal Education? The law is an ever-changing field and any lawyer that does not take significant steps to keep on top of his or her field will soon fall behind the times.

Do You Have a Certified Specialty? Some states permit lawyers to obtain certificates of specialty from the bar association, by proving requisite experience and passing a test. The areas of specialty usually include divorce, workers' compensation, tax, civil, criminal and probate.

How Much Time Are We Talking About? Any legal matter takes time to accomplish. You have the right to the lawyer's best estimate.

You may also have questions of your own to add to this list. In any event, before you leave your interview with each prospective lawyer, you should have a good idea about your case, the likely costs involved, and the time it will take to accomplish. You should also know whether your lawyer seems appropriately experienced and professional to do a good job.

Step 5: Make Your Decision

Once you have done your homework, you should compare and contrast the candidates in your mind to determine which to choose. Think back on your contacts with each lawyer. How well did they appear to know the law? How seriously did they take your concerns? Did they appear willing to treat you with respect? How good were they at communicating? How much will each charge? Give weight to those qualities you deem most important and then make your choice. By going through this detailed process, you will have definitely improved your chances of having a positive experience with your lawyer.

HOW LAWYERS GET PAID

Lawyers charge for their services. (No surprise there.) These charges are known as fees. This is an area of great conflict between lawyers and clients. It's estimated that forty percent of the 100,000 or so consumer complaints about lawyers filed each year with state bar associations are about the fees charged. Miscommunication frequently occurs, so pay special attention when you and the lawyer discuss the issue.

The method and amount of charging fees should be contained in a written contract of representation, known as the *retainer agreement*. (See below.)

There are four main methods of charging, one of which will probably apply in your case:

The Hourly Fee

If you are being charged by the hour, the amount will be established by agreement between you and your lawyer. The charges will be based on hourly increments, usually (15 cents (six minutes). Thus, if your lawyer charges $100 an hour and speaks with you on the telephone for 18 minutes, you will be charged $30 for the service.

Here are some things to keep in mind if you are charged by the hour:

You Have the Right to a Detailed Bill. Do not pay a bill that merely says "$500 for services rendered." (After all, you wouldn't accept a check at a restaurant that asked for "$100 for food eaten.") Such a bill does not tell you what was done, the time it took or the fee for each particular service.

Review the Bill When You Receive It to Make Sure It Is Reasonable. Under an hourly-fee arrangement, the more hours worked, the bigger the bill. That can create an incentive for bill padding or overworking the file. Thus, pay close attention to the bill and be sure to question any charges you deem unreasonable or suspicious.

Beware of Unreasonable Billing Units. Some lawyers offer a low hourly rate and then overcharge by using unreasonable minimum billing units. Thus, if your retainer agreement states that the minimum charge for work on the file is 3/10 hour, beware. That means that even a two-minute telephone call will be charged as if it took 18 minutes.

Find Out If There Is a Retainer Fee. Some lawyers charge an up-front fee (*retainer fee*) to get the case started. This is standard if the fee is considered an advance—that is, hourly fees will be charged against the up-front payment. (Don't be afraid to negotiate over the amount of the up-front fee.) Also, find out whether the retainer fee is refundable if the lawyer finishes the case before using up the advance fee or withdraws from the case before it's completed.

Determine If the Fee Can Be Raised. Some lawyers will take your business, agreeing to charge one hourly fee, and then raise the fee later on. For example, it is standard for lawyers to charge different rates for courtroom litigation and office work. Be sure you understand when and under what circumstances your fee can be raised.

In an hourly fee case, you owe the dough whether you win the case or not. You are also responsible for all out-of-pocket expenses (costs) that are incurred. These costs can be expensive, depending on the kind of case involved, so be sure you get a general estimate up front. Cases that involve hourly fees will probably include divorce, contract representation, will contests, general advice, and representation before government bodies.

The Contingency Fee

Contingency fees are most common in personal injury cases and sometimes can be arranged in wrongful termination cases or some cases against insurance companies. If you win the case, the lawyer will take a percentage of the money actually collected. If you lose, the lawyer gets no fee. (The lawyer can, however, demand reimbursement for costs that may have been fronted for you, known in lawyer-lingo as *advanced costs*.) Contingency fees generally range between twenty-five and forty percent, depending on the complexity of the case and whether it has to go to trial to be resolved.

If you decide to go with a contingency fee, ask that the fee be calculated after cost expenses have been deducted. In that way, the percentage will be based on the net figure, rather than the gross figure. Also, set a limit of expenses you can be billed for. If more expense money is needed after that figure is reached, make sure the lawyer must come to you for approval.

Contingency fees are controversial. Some people claim that they result in a lawyer windfall. This can happen in cases, for example, where one side is clearly wrong and the issue is not whether you will win, but how much you will win. On the other hand, many people could not afford representation, especially against big business interests, without the contingency fee.

Fees Set By Law

The fees that are charged to clients in some areas of the law are set by the legislatures by statute or are left up to judges to decide. For example, when the estate of a deceased person goes through probate, most states set the lawyer's fee based on a percentage of the value of the estate being probated. In other cases, such as disputes with Social Security and workers' compensation, the judge or hearing officer sets the fee. So, too, with conservatorships and guardianships, where the judge sets the attorney's fees depending on the amount of work performed and the size of the estate.

Flat Fees

On occasion, lawyers will quote one pre-established price for the services you want them to render. This is often true of legal clinics, when a lawyer is preparing legal documents such as a will or trust, and in the criminal field. If your lawyer quotes you a flat fee, be sure you get a statement in the retainer that the fee charged is for *everything*, other than costs, or, if additional fees can be charged later, what those fees will be and under what circumstances they can be billed. Also, if your lawyer charges a flat fee, be sure to keep a watchful eye to make sure that no corners are cut.

THE RETAINER AGREEMENT

You should always hire a lawyer using a *written* retainer agreement. In some cases, such as when contingency fees are involved, this is legally required. In others, it is not. Regardless, it is always a good idea to prevent future misunderstandings.

Here are some things to look for in a retainer agreement:

- What the fees will be, how they will be computed, how billed and whether and under what circumstances the fees can be raised
- How costs are to be paid, i.e., do you pay when the fees are due or does the firm advance costs on your behalf
- Which lawyer (in a large firm) will have case responsibility
- Whether the lawyer will use paralegals or less experienced attorneys for certain aspects of your case to save money and what those charges will amount to
- Whether overhead expenses, such as photocopying and parking can be charged to your file, and if so in what amount
- A dispute resolution clause in the agreement to specify how you and your lawyer resolve disputes (Many bar associations have mediation services available which often help attorneys and their clients smooth ruffled feathers.)
- How your lawyer's responsibilities will be established
- How your rights should be set forth, including your right to change lawyers
- Whether your lawyer has an obligation to take the case on appeal should also be established

Written retainer agreements benefit both the client and the lawyer by providing a concrete understanding of the terms of your relationship and the expectations of both sides. Make sure you understand this agreement before signing and take the terms seriously because you are entrusting the attorney with your legal rights.

IF YOU ARE UNHAPPY WITH YOUR LAWYER

When you hire a lawyer, you are putting important matters, perhaps very personal matters, into the hands of someone else and paying them to take care of them for you. That isn't easy under the best of circumstances. However, when you don't believe the lawyer is doing a good job or treating you well, it can be downright devastating and expensive.

If you find yourself in this unhappy state of affairs, here are some things you can do:

Talk to the Lawyer

Lawyers are not mind-readers. They may think they are doing a fine job while you are ready to give them the boot. Your first step, and one that is courteous, is to talk with the lawyer in a calm and reasoned manner and tell him or her why you are unhappy. Since the lawyer wants your business (and your referrals), that should be all it takes. You should back-up your conversation with a friendly letter that memorializes your understanding.

Go to the Top

If you are working with a lawyer who is not an owner of the firm (an associate), you can go to one of the owners (a partner) to tell of your unhappiness and ask for an assignment to a different lawyer. You can also go to a different partner, if the partner lawyer is displeasing you.

Fire Your Lawyer

You have the absolute right to fire your lawyer at any time. However, it is a good idea, especially in litigation matters, to get a new lawyer before you fire your old lawyer. Once you have hired a new lawyer, he or she can take responsibility for informing your old law firm that they are off the case and getting the files transferred.

Sue Your Lawyer

If your lawyer has been negligent in his or her representation and if that negligence has damaged you, you can sue for malpractice. Legal malpractice is a growing area of the law but it can be tough to sue a lawyer, especially in a smaller community, since you may find it difficult to find a malpractice lawyer.* (This

---

* See *If You Want to Sue a Lawyer...A Directory of Legal Malpractice Attorneys*, by Kay Ostberg in association with HALT, Random House,1991. $10.00.

is generally not a big problem in large cities.) In a malpractice claim, you will have two jobs to do:

Prove the Negligence. For your lawyer to have been negligent, his conduct must be below the standard of care in the community. In other words, your lawyer's services must be less than would be provided by a reasonably-competent lawyer under the same circumstances. For example, if your lawyer let a *statute of limitations* run out so that you are legally barred from bringing a lawsuit, that is negligence.

Prove Damages. This may be difficult, even in obvious cases of negligence. In order to prevail in a legal malpractice case, you also have to prove that but for the lawyer's negligence, you would not have been damaged. Thus, if, as in the above example, you are barred from filing suit because of a blown statute of limitations, you must then prove you would have won the case had the lawsuit been filed in a timely manner. Your trial will actually involve two cases—proving the lawyer's negligence and then proving the underlying action.

Arbitrate Fee Disputes

If your dispute with your lawyer involves an argument over the amount of legal fees, you may be able to have the case arbitrated. A little more than half of the state bar associations (and some local bar associations) offer fee arbitration programs—most are voluntary and require the lawyer's permission to proceed (about half a dozen are mandatory and require the lawyer to participate if the client requests arbitration). Arbitration may be binding or nonbinding.

Bar-run arbitration programs have been criticized as being ineffective and partial to attorneys. Reforms that allow nonlawyer arbitrators to participate, that open up hearings to the public and that make all arbitration hearings mandatory on the attorney are improving these systems. For more information, contact your state's program (see Appendix 1).

Report Your Lawyer

If your lawyer has acted unethically, you can report him or her to the state bar association for discipline. Although most complaints are dismissed as misunderstandings or as insufficient enough to raise an ethical concern, sometimes strict action is taken, even disbarment (taking the lawyer's license away).

Every problem you may have with a lawyer may not be appropriate for ethical considerations. However, if any of the following misconduct has occurred, you should take the matter up with the state bar:

- Acts of moral turpitude, such as lying, stealing from you or other acts of dishonesty, such as fraud or misrepresentation
- Mixing your money with the attorney's own funds (known as commingling)
- Acting when there is a conflict of personal, financial or business interest
- Repeated failure to act competently

There are four basic types of discipline:

The Private Reprimand. This is a letter informing the lawyer that he or she acted wrongly and telling them never to do it again (also known as the proverbial slap on the wrist with a ruler). Private reprimands are kept confidential.

The Public Reprimand. This is the same letter published in a bar journal or newspapers. The primary sanction here is the lawyer being embarrassed in front of his or her peers.

Suspension. This can prevent the lawyer from practicing law for a specific period of time.

Disbarment. This takes away the lawyer's right to practice law. Disbarment, because it interferes with the lawyer's right to earn a living, is reserved for the most egregious lapses or for lawyers who have been previously disciplined. Disbarment occurs in less than one percent of all complaints and typically lasts from one to five years before a lawyer can apply for readmission.

Many clients are frustrated by the attorney discipline process. In most states, the proceedings are slow, sometimes taking years, and are conducted in secret. The attorney can usually appeal a decision but the client cannot. Investigative resources are often limited and the reviewing panels in about half the states are composed entirely of lawyers.

Still, if you have been treated unethically, you have a duty to present your case to the bar, if not to help yourself then to prevent another client from being victimized. For more details on the kind of behavior that can give rise to attorney discipline, contact your state bar association. The address and telephone number can be found in Appendix 1.

Note: If you have been the victim of an attorney who stole your money, most states have a *Client Security Trust Fund,* which may be able to fully or partially reimburse you for your out-of-pocket losses. For more information, see Appendix 1.

HOW TO WORK WELL WITH YOUR LAWYER

Here are some things you can do to help your lawyer help you:

Communicate Openly and Honestly. It is important to let your lawyer know the truth about your case since it will affect his or her recommendations and analysis. (Your lawyer must keep what you say confidential by law. However, if you sue for malpractice, you give up the right to confidentiality as it relates to the issues of the malpractice case.)

Do What You Promise. If you have committed yourself to doing certain tasks, perform them completely and promptly. After all, if you don't take your case seriously, your lawyer may be less likely to as well.

Keep Your Lawyer Informed. This means updating the lawyer on events that affect your case. It also means letting your lawyer know if you omitted any important information in prior consultations.

Pay Your Lawyer. If your lawyer performs properly, he or she has the right to be paid for the services pursuant to your retainer agreement. This is not only common courtesy but enlightened self-interest. While lawyers are not ethically permitted to stop work on cases just because they have not been paid, it sure takes the wind out of their sails. Moreover, if you don't pay, they can eventually kick you out of the office, either by telling you to pack up your files and leave (giving you a reasonable time to find other representation), or, in the case of litigation, filing a motion in court to be relieved as counsel of record.

Show Appreciation. Lawyers are human. A pat on the back for a job well done is always appreciated and is likely to renew their enthusiasm for your cause.

10

PATIENT'S RIGHTS

The law affects nearly every aspect of our lives, including our dealings with doctors and hospitals. How we choose to deal with doctors impacts the level and type of care we receive and the cost. Much is at stake: your health, both physical and financial.

This chapter will explore the physician/patient relationship. We will discuss how to find a doctor, your rights as a patient, and your rights if you are hospitalized. We will also describe how your health care is impacted by different types of health insurance, including traditional fee-for-service insurance versus health maintenance organizations.

FINDING A DOCTOR

Good medical care starts with finding a good doctor. Unless you have a specific malady that you want treated, you should probably begin by finding a primary care physician. A primary care physician is the current term for the good ol' GP (General Practitioner), a doctor who can take care of most of your needs and, if necessary, refer you to a specialist. (Actually, the last sentence is technically inaccurate. Today, primary care physicians *are* specialists.)

There are three principal types of doctors who act as primary care doctors: internists, family practitioners and pediatricians.

Internists. Internists practice in the discipline of internal medicine; that is, they diagnose and give medical (nonsurgical) treatments to adults.

Family Practitioner. A family practitioner is a doctor who practices general family care. He or she will have training in internal medicine, general surgery, obstetrics and gynecology, pediatrics and psychiatry.

Pediatrician. Pediatricians care for and treat children from birth through the teens or early twenties.

Finding the right doctor is a process similar to selecting the right lawyer. Here is a step-by-step approach:

Step 1: Get Referrals

Getting the names of good doctors is important. There are several places to look:

Other Doctors. Doctors generally know who are the best physicians in their community. This is especially true if you need a referral to a specialist, such as a cardiologist or an orthopedic surgeon. (One of the jobs of your primary care physician is as a referral source to the specialists.)

Some doctors refer to others based on reasons other than medical excellence. For example, it may be seen as a social obligation or as part of a mutual referral society. That is not the kind of referral you want. Thus, when a doctor refers you to a colleague, be sure to ask *why* the doctor believes this person is the best physician for you.

Nurses and Other Medical Personnel. The support staff in the field of medicine sees a lot of what goes on behind the scenes. Not only that, they tend to talk to each other about the good, the bad and the ugly ongoing in the health-care scene. Thus, they too are likely to know the better physicians from those doctors who are best avoided.

Friends and Family. Other consumers, in this case patients, are usually reliable sources of referrals. As with lawyers, referrals from satisfied patients are a major way doctors build their practices. So, if you are in the market for a new doctor, conduct your own mini-market survey to enhance your chances of finding a good doctor.

Local Medical Societies. Your local medical association is made up of doctors who live and practice locally. While the association's primary responsibility is to serve the needs of its members, many associations have computerized referral services available to you for little or no cost. The referral will usually consist of three names of doctors who are close to you and who practice in your area of need. The referral can also tell you where each doctor attended medical school and give a list of credentials (see below).

Hospitals. Hospitals aggressively market themselves as a normal part of business activities. One form of marketing is a physician referral service wherein referrals are made to doctors on staff at the hospital. This can help you, since it can give you the name of a good doctor, and it helps the hospital since if you ever need to be hospitalized, guess which hospital your doctor will probably want to admit you to?

Local Referral Services. Many areas have local referral services. The level of pre-screening will vary. Usually doctors have to pay to be on the list or the service is paid by hospitals who use the referral service as a means of garnering business.

HMO Referrals. If you are a member of an HMO, you are restricted to the doctors on the HMO-approved list. Still, you will want to follow the same steps when deciding on the primary care physician who will serve as your "gatekeeper." (See below.)

Step 2: Research the Candidates

There is a lot of information you need to know about the doctor you select to take care of you. This includes the answers to the following questions:

What Are the Doctor's Credentials? This is an area where the proper terminology is important. Don't ask, "What is the doctor's specialty?" Once licensed, a doctor can "specialize" in any area of health care, regardless of background and training (or the lack thereof). For example, in one notorious case, a doctor trained as an obstetrician held himself out as a "specialist" in plastic surgery. (You can guess the unfortunate results.)

The proper question to ask is, "Are you *Board Certified* in _____ (e.g., internal medicine, hematology, etc.)?" A doctor who is board certified has completed residency training in a specific specialty (residency training comes after internship and can last several years) and passed examinations designed to test his or her knowledge of that specialty. A doctor who has passed the test is called board certified. A doctor who has sufficient training and experience to take the test (or who may have failed the test) is called board qualified. Your best bet is to get at least a board certified physician.

There are other credentials of note. For example, some physicians receive recognition from their colleagues, usually for research or other intellectual endeavors. This recognition is known as a "fellowship." You can tell whether a doctor is a Fellow by initials that will appear on his or her business card, for example: Wesley J. Smith, M.D. F.A.C.S. which would stand for Wesley J. Smith, Medical Doctor, Fellowship of the American College of Surgeons. (In my mother's dreams.)

Where Does the Doctor Have Staff Privileges? Every doctor cannot admit patients into every hospital. To do so, the doctor must pass peer review muster and be accepted as a member of the hospital's staff. Be wary of a doctor that does not have admitting privileges somewhere.

What Is the Doctor's Policy Regarding Insurance? Some doctors will take what insurance pays as payment in full while others will not. Likewise, some doctors will cost Medicare recipients less than others by "accepting the assignment" (taking what Medicare offers as a reasonable fee as the actual fee charged.) If such financial issues are important to you, be sure to find the answers to such questions before beginning treatment.*

---

* For more information on the rights of medicare recipients, see HALT's book, *Legal Rights for Seniors,* by Wesley J. Smith. $10.

Once you are satisfied that you have a doctor that appears to be the right one, you should meet the physician to make sure. To do this, make an appointment for a physical or ask for a short consultation. The doctor may charge you but in the long run it will be money well spent to make sure that the doctor lives up to your expectations.

YOUR RIGHTS AS A PATIENT

When you are under a doctor's care, you have some very important rights. These rights are designed to protect your dignity, your privacy and ensure your ability to receive the level of care *you* choose.

The Right to Confidentiality

Your health care is extremely personal. This truth is recognized in the law and in the canons of medical ethics. Thus, doctors and their medical staffs cannot disclose information about your medical condition to others except under very limited circumstances. Those circumstances are as follows:

If You Sue Your Doctor For Medical Malpractice. If you sue your doctor, your confidentiality rights are waived so far as the information is relevant to the lawsuit.

If Your Health Becomes an Issue in a Lawsuit. When you sue or are sued, you lose your right to confidentiality if your health is an issue in the suit. This is particularly true in personal injury cases.

If You Suffer From a Reportable Condition. Society's need to effectively fight communicable diseases overrides the right to confidentiality in specific circumstances. Thus, if you have a disease such as syphilis, your doctor is duty-bound to report that to the state board of health so that action can be taken to prevent the spread of the disease. (There are over 50 reportable conditions, including anthrax, botulism, gonorrhea, hepatitis, typhus, whooping cough and AIDS.) However, your right to confidentiality vis-à-vis the rest of the world is not affected and you have the right to confidentiality with regard to HIV testing. (Being HIV+ is not a reportable condition.)

The Right to Informed Consent

When your doctor tells you that you need medical treatment, diagnostic tests, or other medical procedures performed, it doesn't mean you have to follow his or her advice. The final say in such issues is yours, under a legal doctrine know as *informed consent.*

The bottom line of informed consent is that your permission must be based on a full disclosure of relevant facts, such as the pros and cons of going forward with the medical procedure, the possible consequences of not going forward and any alternatives that might be available.

If doctors don't encourage informed consent, they expose themselves to malpractice claims if something goes wrong that you were not advised might occur. Failure to fully advise you concerning your health care decisions may also be an ethical violation, which, if severe, might impact the doctor's license.

The Right to Informed Refusal

The flip side of informed consent is your right to refuse treatment. This is known as *informed refusal.* Under the doctrine of informed refusal you have the right to refuse medical treatment, medical tests, surgery or any other procedure, so long as you are competent to make the decision and the refusal is informed. You can even leave a hospital against your doctor's orders.

The issue of informed refusal has become controversial in the area of refusing life-prolonging medical intervention, known popularly as "extraordinary care." For example, if you are terminally ill, you can refuse all treatment. Or, you can opt for hospice care rather than curative medical treatment. (Hospice care offers compassion and dignity for those suffering from terminal conditions, as well as the person's family. Hospice care is not designed to cure disease or prolong life but, rather, to make life as comfortable and meaningful as possible.)

The right to refuse care can extend to times when you are incompetent—if you have prepared what is known as an advance medical directive such as a living will, or durable power of attorney for health care (DPOA). For information on the benefits of advance directives, contact: Choice In Dying, 200 Varick St., New York, NY 10014. For information on some of the pitfalls of advance directives, contact: International Anti-Euthanasia Task Force, P.O. Box 760, Steubenville, OH 43952.

The Right to a Second Opinion

You have the right to get a second opinion if you are unsure of your doctor's diagnosis. This issue usually comes up if your doctor recommends surgery or rigorous medical treatment. However, you may also want a second opinion even if your doctor gives you a clean bill of health, since sometimes doctors misdiagnose by not recognizing medical conditions that are really there. (There have been studies that show that women's health complaints receive less serious consideration by some doctors than the complaints of men.)

Second opinions may also be important to your pocketbook. Many insurance companies pay only limited benefits if you fail to obtain a second opinion before non-emergency surgery or hospitalization, while paying full benefits if you do. You can save yourself literally thousands of dollars by getting a second opinion. Be sure and check your insurance policy for details on your second opinion obligation.

The Right to Continuity of Care

Once you have been accepted by a doctor as his or her patient, the relationship cannot be terminated at the doctor's whim. (It can be at yours.) Generally, a doctor can only stop treating you if you no longer need further care or if you have had the opportunity to find replacement care of equal quality. To do otherwise is to abandon you, which can lead to an ethical sanction against the doctor or a medical malpractice claim if the abandonment injures you.

The Right to Copies of Your File

Many doctors do not encourage their patients to keep copies of their own medical files. Happily, the decision isn't the doctor's. In most states, you have the legal right to demand copies of your own medical records at any time.

This can be important for several reasons: You may decide to change doctors and giving the doctor your up-to-date records can be very helpful. Or, you may want a second opinion and the second doctor will need to see the records. (The second opinion doctor can also get them from your doctor if you sign an authorization.) Or, you may feel malpractice has occurred and want to show the records to a lawyer or doctor giving an opinion on that topic. Or, you may just want to have them, since they are about you.

HOSPITALS

All hospitals are not created equal. Some do a better job of keeping you comfortable, some a better job of reducing the risk of secondary infection, and some have better mortality rates than others or are better equipped for specific types of care. That being so, if you have a choice of hospitals in your area (you may not in an HMO setting or a small community), finding the right hospital is key to maintaining your health.

The primary element that goes into choosing a hospital is your admitting doctor's referral. (Under normal circumstances, only doctors on staff at a hospital can admit you to that hospital.) Even so, you should take the time to discuss the issue to make sure the hospital being recommended is the best in the community for your type of problem, and not being recommended merely because it is close to the doctor's office.

You should also research the hospital you will be entering. Ask to see the hospital's Joint Commission on the Accreditation of Health Care Organizations (JCAHO) rating. The JCAHO is a private organization that inspects hospitals and issues accreditations ranging from probation to three years. The JCAHO accrediting report is available for you to read, detailing what the Commission liked and didn't like about the hospital. Ask the administration to see it if you have any concerns about the quality of the hospital.

You should also contact the State Health Department to see if it has received serious complaints about the facility. (The Health Department is the licensing agency for the hospital.) If both the JCAHO and Health Department appear approving of the hospital, chances are it is a quality facility. Remember, before being admitted to a hospital (except in an emergency) be sure it is approved by your health insurance plan. Otherwise, you may not receive full benefits.

Your Rights in a Hospital

Your state law will detail your legal rights as a patient in a hospital. These will probably include the following:

- You have the right to exercise your rights without regard to sex, cultural, economic, educational or religious background or the source of payment for your care.
- You have the right to be treated with respect and consideration by all hospital personnel.
- You have the right to know the physician in charge of coordinating your care (called the attending physician) and the names and professional relationships of other physicians who will consult with the attending physician.
- You have the right to give your informed consent or informed refusal (see above).
- You have the right to continuity of care.
- You have the right to be advised if your care will be given in conjunction with a medical research project and to refuse to participate in the experimental care, if you desire.
- You have a right to a clear, easy-to-understand, detailed bill, regardless of the source of payment.
- You have the right to know the rules and hospital policies that apply to your conduct as a patient.

You should also be ready to enforce your rights. The first step to solving problems is to talk with the staff person creating the difficulty (or having a family member or friend do it for you). If that doesn't work, follow the chain of command up to administration. Most hospitals have an administrator or other staff person whose sole job it is to deal with patient complaints. (The extension number of the patient-problem solver is available upon request or can be found in the informational documents you will receive upon admission to the hospital.) You should also tell the physician who admitted you since hospitals want to keep their doctors happy (and keep those admissions rolling in).

Once you are out of the hospital, you can complain to the powers-that-be. The address of your state health department will be in the telephone book. The JCAHO can be reached at 1 Renaissance Blvd., Oakbrook, IL 60181, telephone (708) 916-5600.

Dealing With Your Bill

Most hospitals charge for every item and service they provide *a la carte*, that is, you are billed for everything you use on an individualized basis (other than the bed, basic care and nursing services, which are covered in the price per day). Thus, use two aspirin and you will be charged for two aspirin, (probably at the price of a whole bottle). Even the shortest stay in a hospital will likely produce a huge bill, probably several pages in length.

Seeing such a long and detailed bill can be daunting. How are you to know whether the charges are true? (A lot of people and insurance companies are overcharged by hospitals. This is usually unintentional but still, money is money.) However, there is a tool at your disposal. If you believe you have been over-charged for any reason, you have the right to ask for a chart audit. A chart audit involves a comparison of your medical bill with your actual medical chart. Mistakes that are caught are corrected. (You should send a copy of the request to your insurance company.)

IF SOMETHING GOES WRONG

If you are unhappy with your doctor, you have rights that can be enforced. They can be summarized as follows:

Talk to Your Doctor

The first place to go with any consumer complaint is the source; in this case, your doctor. When discussing the matter with your doctor be sure to be specific. Let the doctor know why you are unhappy and see if the matter can be resolved between you. (Put your complaints into a politely-worded letter to the doctor, keeping a copy for your records.)

Change Doctors

If you no longer trust your doctor or wish the doctor to handle your care, you have the right to make a switch. If you are going to do so, be sure to work within the rules of your health insurance plan. (Many policies require you to choose from a doctor on their list.) You should also make sure your continuity of care is maintained. In other words, don't give the first doctor the boot until you have your new one on board ready to provide you with medical care.

Seek Out Peer Review

Relatively minor patient problems are often handled by regional medical associations for their members. This can bring some pressure to bear on your doctor, which can be helpful. However, peer review is really a paper tiger and your doctor knows it. The most that a peer group can do is kick your doctor out of the voluntary professional association, which is rarely done, and, in any event, peer review procedures have no effect on their license. And the pressure of peers only works if your doctor cares about what his or her colleagues think. Unfortunately, not all doctors do.

Report Your Doctor

Like lawyers, doctors are licensed by the state. Unlike lawyers, the state medical licensing board will usually handle ethical complaints, as opposed to a peer association.

The following are acts that may trigger state disciplinary action against a doctor:

- Incompetence
- Gross negligence
- Repeated negligent acts

- Falsifying medical records
- Fraudulent medical bill claims
- Mental or physical illness that substantially impairs a doctor's ability to practice medicine safely
- Abuse of drugs or alcohol
- Prescribing drugs without a medical exam
- Sexual relations with a patient

If you have suffered one of these wrongs, you should report your doctor to the state. At that point, they will begin an investigation. However, unless the matter is considered an emergency, don't expect much to happen fast. Even if the state board decides to take up the matter, which is relatively rare, you can expect long, bureaucratic delays and legal appeals that can go on for years. (It isn't a pretty picture.) Except in the worst cases, you will probably be referred back to peer review, which, as was previously discussed, isn't worth much unless your doctor really cares.

Medical Malpractice

If your doctor has treated you negligently, you can sue. However, most suits are hard to bring, since there are limits imposed by law in most states on damages that can be collected and on the amount of the contingency fee a lawyer can charge. That may make it difficult to find a lawyer (which is the point of the law). In addition, you (or your lawyer) will also have to find a doctor willing to testify against a colleague, which also may not be easy. (This is often called the "conspiracy of silence.") Finally, if you are in an HMO, the terms of your contract with the HMO may require you to seek arbitration instead of litigation.

For more information on medical malpractice law in your state, consult with a lawyer who specializes in the field. They will usually give a no-cost initial interview and take the case on a contingency fee if they deem the case worthy, which usually means they think that you have a good chance of winning your case and that the attorney can make a large fee.

THE HMO DIFFERENCE

All medicine used to be provided by what is called "fee-for-service" methods. That is, you received a service and then paid for it.

Then health insurance was created and the complications began. For decades, the fee-for-service system remained intact: you received medical treatment and your health insurance paid for it, subject to your obligation to pay a modest up-front portion of the cost of care (called the *deductible*), and thereafter, a percentage of the cost of care (called the *copayment*.) Usually you were responsible for twenty percent and the insurance company eighty percent.

Then, for reasons beyond the scope of this book, the cost of medicine skyrocketed. So did health insurance premiums. That led to innovations in the ways in which health insurance worked. These innovations, generally under the term "cost containment," primarily come in two variations: restrictions in the fee for service policy, and the health maintenance organization (HMO).

Cost Containment and Fee-For-Service Health Insurance

Fee-for-service remains the method by which most people receive their health insurance. However, certain restrictions have been implemented in most policies to control insurance company costs., that you should be aware of:

Preferred Provider Organization (PPO). If you are part of a PPO, you receive full benefits only if you use those health care providers and hospitals identified by your health insurance company as being preferred providers. Use other than preferred providers and the health insurance company will pay reduced benefits.

Second Guessing. You and your doctor no longer have unlimited discretion in determining your health care needs.

Rather, you will have to receive permission from your health insurance carrier before undertaking certain care (except in emergencies). Thus, if your doctor wants to put you in the hospital, the health insurance company must be advised first to make sure they will pay the tab. So too with nonemergency surgery, certain diagnostic tests and the length of hospital stay.

That isn't all. Health insurance companies now reserve the right to determine the appropriateness of your care, and the reasonableness of its cost after the care has been rendered. If they deem the treatment unnecessary, they will not pay for it. If they think the price for the care is too expensive, they will only pay that portion the insurance company deems just and reasonable, leaving you responsible for the balance of the cost.

Insurance companies also control costs by excluding people with previous health problems from coverage or excluding preexisting conditions from coverage. That has left a lot of people either uninsured or underinsured.

Despite these innovations, the cost of fee-for-service health insurance remains incredibly high. That has led to a movement toward the HMO.

Health Maintenance Organization

In a health maintenance organization, you get substantially all of your health care (there may be very small copayments) for the cost of your insurance premium, which is less expensive than a fee for service insurance premium. Not only that: the cost of prescriptions and preventive care is often covered by HMOs when they are often excluded in fee for service policies. (Unlike fee for service insurance, HMOs emphasize preventive care as a form of cost control and a way to keep you healthier.)

Under an HMO, you must usually use the doctors and hospitals who are authorized by the HMO. (That may be a large group or a small number of doctors, depending on the HMO.) If you go outside the system, you may not be covered or covered only at 80 percent.

The quality of care provided by HMOs varies. Some consumers rave about their care in an HMO while others complain that it is harder to get appointments, necessary medical tests or referrals to specialists in an HMO setting. One thing is clear: The emphasis HMOs place on early detection and treatment can reduce health care costs by preventing the need for long-term hospitalization.

This chapter has only touched the surface of many important consumer issues relating to health care. For more information on such issues, you might consider joining the People's Medical Society, a non-profit organization dedicated to promoting the rights of health care consumers. They can be reached at 462 Walnut St., Allentown, PA 18102, telephone (610) 770-1670. The cost of membership is $20 a year, for which you will receive a newsletter every other month. The Society also has an extensive list of books on health care and your rights as a consumer.

11

PURCHASING INSURANCE

Insurance is a big business. In the United States alone there are approximately 5,800 insurance companies that generate premiums of over $600 billion for all types of insurance. According to the National Insurance Consumer Organization, the average American family spends almost $3,000 every year in out-of-pocket premiums and about $4,500 in indirect payments (insurance paid by employers or by businesses with the cost passed through to consumers in the price of goods.) This amounts to approximately twelve percent of the disposable income in the United States. In fact, Americans pay more for insurance than they do for federal income taxes, not counting Social Security.

This chapter will address the legal issues you need to know about with regard to most types of personal insurance policies (nonbusiness insurance you purchase as an individual or to protect your family). Among the topics addressed will be: the anatomy of an insurance policy, the difference between cash value and term life insurance, the law that permits laid-off workers and divorcing spouses to keep employer-provided health insurance, and the methods policyholders can use to enforce their rights.

THE ANATOMY OF AN INSURANCE POLICY

An insurance policy is a legal contract. Like any contract, both parties involved have certain rights and obligations. For your part, you have to pay premiums, file any claims in the appropriate manner, and, if there is a dispute, attempt to resolve it (at least initially) as provided in the contract itself, the insurance policy. In turn, the insurance company must pay benefits (either directly to you or to a third party, such as a doctor) if you suffer damages as defined in the policy.

The details of both your rights and obligations will be found in the terms of the policy. If you have not read your policy, you should. If you don't understand the language, ask your agent to explain the wording or get someone with a good grasp of understanding complex writing. There may be terms that you were not aware of which add to the rights you believe you have in the policy, or which unexpectedly take some rights away you would otherwise enjoy. (With insurance, *it is what you don't know that can hurt you.* You may think you are covered and then, when you suffer a loss, find out that you are not.) As a result, insurance holders may not always know the hazards they are protected against, and, perhaps more importantly, what hazards are not covered by insurance.

The following questions must be answered if you are to know what your rights are vis-à-vis your own insurance company:

What Is Covered?

To find out what is covered in your insurance policy, turn to the endorsements section, usually found on the front page or often sent separately from the actual policy upon renewal. The endorsements page is a summary of the policy—it provides an overview, the level of coverage and the like, but it does not contain the details (sometimes known as the "fine print"), which are located in the agreement section of the policy. Thus, you will need to read both the endorsements section and agreement section to understand the exact nature of your coverage.

You will find the following information on your endorsements page:

- The name and address of the insurance company
- The type of policy
- The name and address of the insured
- The exact time the policy is in effect
- The extent of coverage (limits, deductibles, etc.)
- Whether you have purchased extra coverage, called a rider or endorsement, depending on the type of policy you have purchased

For example, say your auto insurance policy provides that the policy is in effect from 12:01 A.M. on January 10, 1994, until July 9, 1994, at midnight. If you are in an accident during that time period and the damages are covered by the terms of the policy, your company must pay benefits. However, if the accident happens even minutes outside the time of coverage, the company probably will have no obligation. For that reason, it is important to keep your insurance continually in effect.

What Isn't Covered?

Every policy will restrict the scope of coverage by removing areas of risk that would otherwise come under the insurance umbrella. These are known as *exclusions.* (For example, a standard homeowner's insurance policy excludes earthquake damage from coverage. In order to be protected from damage caused by an earthquake, you will have to pay for extra coverage.) The exclusions section is one of the most important in the policy. If you don't understand what is excluded, you may later discover that you will have to pay for a loss out of your pocket when you thought the insurance company was behind you.

How Do I Know What the Words of the Policy Mean?

The meaning of words can differ, depending on who is doing the interpretation. Since insurance companies don't want a court interpreting the words of the policy—perhaps in a way that will cost them money—every insurance policy will have a definitions section that will define what certain words mean so that there is no doubt.

Even seemingly simple words can have a special meaning in an insurance contract. For example, assume you have a policy which states that it protects you "from liability for damages caused to others by your negligence." Assume further that you live with your adult son. Then assume that the policy contains the typical policy definition: "Throughout this policy 'you' and 'your' refers to (1), The named insured on the declarations page, and (2), the spouse if a resident of the same household."

Under this policy, your son would *not* be covered under your homeowner's policy, even though he was a family member and lived in your household. Under such conditions, extra coverage would have to be purchased to bring your son under the umbrella of your homeowner's policy.

How Do I Make a Claim?

The manner in which you make a claim with your insurance company will be set forth in the policy. This too must be read and understood, because failure to comply with the proper procedure could delay payment.

THE CLAIMS PROCESS

Filing claims can be an exasperating experience, even when things go smoothly. Still, by doing the job right, you are more likely to receive relatively prompt payment that reasonably compensates you for your damages. It is important to note that for most claims it is not necessary to hire an attorney to represent you, either with your own insurer or with the insurer of someone who has injured you. This is especially true for matters that are not complicated or which don't involve a high level of damages. However, that may not be true in more complicated cases, such as if the insurance company denies coverage or the matter involves severe injuries.

Generally, here's how the claims process works:

You file a claim, using the claims form provided by the company. It is best to type the form, but, at the very least, make sure the claim is well organized and legible. Remember, the claim you submit will be the first impression the claims adjuster will have of you and you want to make a respectable impression.

Your claim is sent to the claims adjuster, usually but not always an employee of your insurance company.

The adjuster then investigates the claim. During this process, you may be asked to send documents, pictures, estimates or other evidence to verify your claim. Or, the adjuster may come to inspect the damage or speak with you personally.

Once the claim has been investigated, you will be made an offer of settlement or your claim will be rejected. You and the adjuster may negotiate and finally come to an agreement. Beware of being "low-balled," that is, being offered a settlement that is materially lower than the claim is actually worth. (You may want to get some independent estimates about costs to make sure you are treated fairly.)

Once you and the adjuster reach agreement, you will be asked to sign a release. A signed release terminates all further claims or rights you may have against the insurance company, even if you later find out that you were owed more money. Or to put it another way, once you sign the release and take the claim money, it is considered payment in full.

If your claim is rejected, and you believe you are being treated wrongly, you will have to take steps to enforce the policy provisions (see below).

Note: There is usually a deadline by which you must file claims or the insurance company is off the hook. Be sure you understand these time factors so you are not left out in the cold.

Enforcing Your Claim

If you are dissatisfied with the adjuster's offer of settlement or if your claim is rejected, you will have to take action. Here are your options:

Pursue Policy Remedies. The adjuster's decision is not necessarily the last word on the subject of the claim. Insurance companies always have an internal process whereby you can pursue your claim when you and the adjuster cannot agree. For example, the matter may be handled informally by meeting with the adjuster's superiors and/or writing a letter of complaint. That may be sufficient to have the matter formally reviewed by company higher-ups, after which you may receive a more appropriate settlement.

If that doesn't work, you should refer to the policy to see what remedies are found in the contract to settle disputes. Often, arbitration is the method provided for in the policy contract. Some arbitration clauses are stacked in favor of the insurance company, which is not surprising since the company's lawyers wrote the terms of the policy. (For details on how arbitration works, see Chapter 3.)

File a Lawsuit. If the dispute with the company remains unsettled after pursuing policy remedies, the only way to force your insurance company to perform is to sue it. (Some policies preclude this by making arbitration the policyholder's sole remedy.) The lawsuit will usually charge the company with *breach of contract;* that is, the company will be charged with breaking its promises made in the insurance policy. The remedy for breach of contract is restricted to forcing the company to pay the money that is owed. (In other words, there will be no compensation for your emotional suffering or any chance to obtain *punitive damages.*)

Sometimes an insurance company's conduct in denying a valid claim is so outrageous that you may be able to sue the company for more than breach of contract. These suits are known as *bad faith cases.* If successful, bad faith cases permit you to be paid more than the amount that was owed, and to compensate you for other damages. You may also be entitled to punitive damages, a money award designed to punish the company for intentional and malicious wrongdoing and to deter other companies from acting in a similar wrongful manner. Bad faith cases are relatively rare but they can be brought under particularly egregious circumstances. (Unfortunately, because of a United States Supreme Court decision, you can't bring bad faith cases against health insurance companies when health insurance is a benefit of employment.)

In real life, it is difficult to sue insurance companies. First, you may have to hire a lawyer and pay court costs, which will not be cheap. (Even if your case is taken under a contingency fee arrangement, you may be responsible for costs.) Second, insurance companies are rich, powerful institutions. If you choose to fight, the cost and time spent in the litigation may cause you to decide not to pursue your rights. That is why many policyholders settle for less than they may be entitled to. (If the claim is relatively small, consider taking the case to small claims court. It's cheap, it's fast and the vast power of the insurance company will not be able to be used to bog you down.)

Report the Company. Insurance companies are regulated by each state. This regulatory scheme allows you another avenue of redress when the company doesn't pay benefits or cancels a policy without legal justification.

State insurance departments act as insurance cops on the beat and investigate many consumer complaints, including:

- Improper denial of claims
- Unreasonable delays in settling claims
- Illegal cancellation or termination of policies
- Misappropriation of funds paid in trust to an agent or broker
- Premium disputes, such as a raise without apparent cause

If you have such a complaint, contact your state insurance department (its number will be in the telephone book under state government listings), and ask for a complaint form. Fill it out carefully and be sure to document your complaint as completely as possible. (Be sure and fill out the complaint form pursuant to instructions. Otherwise, the bureaucrats at the agency may send it back to you.) Also be sure to send a copy of the complaint to the insurance company. The mere act of complaining to the regulatory agency is often enough to break the impasse between you and your company.

Guarantee Funds. Unfortunately, from time to time insurance companies go out of business or otherwise become insolvent. This can leave you holding a very big financial bag.

Most states cushion such blows through guarantee funds. Money in the funds come from the insurance companies themselves. The funds will pay for most benefits that would otherwise be lost. Any questions about guarantee funds should be directed to your state insurance department.

THE INS AND OUTS OF SPECIFIC POLICIES

Beyond the generic issues you need to be concerned about with every insurance policy, there are some specific concerns you should be aware of regarding insurance. An overview of the different kinds of insurance will be discussed in the rest of this chapter.

Health Insurance

Health insurance may be the most important type of insurance you can obtain for the protection of you and your family. We have already touched upon a few of the important issues involving health insurance in the last chapter. But there is more to discuss.

Obtaining Health Insurance. Unless you are young, healthy, employed by a large employer or are a member of a large union, health insurance may be difficult to obtain. That is because health insurance companies "cherry pick;" that is, they seek to insure healthy and young people while denying coverage to older people or those with a history of health problems. This often means that people with chronic conditions, such as diabetes, or people who have survived life-threatening diseases, such as cancer or heart ailments, cannot obtain insurance.

If you are uninsured, your only hope of "affordable" health insurance may be to become a member of a large group of people that uses the clout of numbers to purchase health insurance for every member of the group (thus the term, *group policy*.) Large groups are often insured, regardless of the condition of individual members. Thus, if you're looking for employment, you may want to focus on jobs with large employers that offers group coverage as a benefit. (You may also be forced to stay in a job you don't like in order to keep coverage.) Or, you may want to join an organization, such as a trade group or advocacy group, that offers access to group coverage.

Preexisting Condition Exclusions. Some companies will allow you to purchase insurance but will not cover you for conditions that you had prior to obtaining the policy. Sometimes the exclusion will be for a defined period of time, say six months. In other policies, it may be forever. In any event, be sure you understand the exact terms of preexisting condition exclusions in your policy.

Waiting Periods. Often there are waiting periods before health insurance goes into effect. Any medical bills incurred during this period will not be covered.

Types of Treatment. Health insurance usually excludes from coverage "nontraditional treatment" such as chiropractic treatment or acupuncture. Mental health counselling is often also excluded (but not psychiatric care of a diagnosed illness, such as depression).

Portability. In the ongoing debate about reforming health care in the United States, one thing virtually everyone agrees with is: Health insurance needs to be portable—that is, you should be able to take your coverage with you if you change a job, move, etc. Hopefully, this means that preexisting exclusion clauses and waiting periods will soon be a thing of the past.

There is a law already in effect that allows limited portability. It is known as COBRA (for Congressional Omnibus Budget Reconciliation Act). COBRA protects the health insurance coverage of laid-off workers, divorced and widowed spouses of covered workers, and others from losing their health insurance benefits. The law provides that laid-off workers may, at their own expense, convert their group coverage from work to a policy in their own name for a period of 18 months. Divorced and widowed spouses are similarly protected for three years, as are children who have become adults and therefore have ceased to be protected by their parents' group policy.

The benefits of COBRA are many:

- No preexisting condition clauses or waiting periods exist, because the insurance never lapses.
- The premium will be lower, because it will be computed at the group rate rather than the more expensive individual rate.
- Treatment being received can continue without interruption.

Auto Insurance

Everyone who owns a car is required by law in each state to have auto insurance or some other proof of financial responsibility, such as a bond. The law notwithstanding, and as the potential costs of an accident are quite high, it is important for everyone who owns or leases a car to have their automobile insured.

The typical automobile insurance policy consists of the following:

Liability Protection. This part of the policy protects the policyholder from liability for bodily injury that might be caused to others due to negligent driving. The policy will usually have a split-limit amount, such as $50,000/$100,000. The first figure represents the maximum each injured person is entitled to receive from the insurance company no matter how severely injured, and the latter figure the maximum amount the company will pay per accident, no matter how many people are injured, or how severe their injuries. Most states set the minimum amount of liability insurance you must have (or other form of protection, such as a bond) at $15,000/$30,000, although some require higher coverage and some lower. (Ask your insurance agent for the minimum requirements in your state.)

Property Damage. This portion of the policy compels the insurance company to pay for property damaged by the policyholder, such as another car or a fence. Like the coverage for personal injury, the policy will provide maximum benefits that the insurance company has to pay. Many states require minimum coverage of $10,000 or so, but in this age where even the least expensive cars can cost $10,000, that may not be enough to fully protect your assets.

Cost of Defense. The liability portion of the policy also requires that the company pay for the lawyers and court costs if you are sued.

Medical Pay. This optional coverage pays for the medical bills (and funeral expenses) of the insured, his or her family, or a passenger in the insured's car that is injured or killed in an accident. The medical pay portion pays benefits regardless of fault.

Uninsured Motorist. This optional coverage protects the insured for personal injury damages caused by an uninsured (or in some cases, underinsured) driver. This protection is based on fault. If you are insured and you cause the accident with the uninsured driver, the company will deny your claim (but will have to defend you if you are sued by the uninsured driver and pay claims up to the policy limits). Uninsured motorist is important protection, seeing that fully one-third of all drivers on the road in some areas of the country have no auto insurance.

Uninsured motorist protection has a split-limit similar to liability coverage. To collect benefits for injuries caused by an uninsured driver, you must make a claim against your own policy. Thereafter, if there is a dispute, the matter will be resolved by arbitration. If you end up in a knockdown, drag-out fight over what you are owed, you may wish to consider retaining a personal injury lawyer.

Collision and Comprehensive Coverage. Collision protects the insured's vehicle for the cost of repairs or a payment equivalent to the fair market value of the vehicle, when it is involved in an accident. This coverage is not based on fault. (Collision coverage is optional. Many people with older cars do not take out the coverage because the benefits paid under the policy would be too low to justify the premiums.)

Comprehensive coverage is similar to collision coverage except it protects against losses such as theft, damage from falling objects and other such occurrences. It too is optional and not based on fault. Both collision and comprehensive require a *deductible.* The higher the deductible (the part you pay) the lower the premiums.

A word about no-fault insurance: Fourteen states have some version of "no-fault" insurance. No-fault is designed to reduce court congestion and the price of auto insurance by eliminating smaller cases from the court system. The idea is for everyone who has been injured to receive benefits from his or her own insurance company for lost wages and medical bills, quickly, from their own company, whether or not he or she caused the accident. In return, the insured gives up the right to sue in small cases and the right to receive dollar payments to compensate for pain and suffering - damages that are collectable in fault cases.

Auto insurance policies in fault and no-fault states are similar, although no-fault insurance will have a personal injury policy section (PIP) that defines the company's obligations in the event a no-fault claim is made. People still need liability coverage because larger accidents do not come under the no-fault provision of the law. Also, in most no-fault states, property damage issues remain under the fault system.

Homeowner's Insurance

Homeowner's insurance is designed to protect homeowners from damage to property and personal liability for negligence.

Five basic areas are typically protected in the property section of a homeowner's policy:

- The dwelling
- Other structures on the property
- Personal property
- Loss of use
- Miscellaneous coverages

Homeowner's policies protect against damage caused by fire, lightning, windstorm, theft, riot, vandalism and damage caused by vehicles. The basic policy may or may not cover losses due to the weight of snow, falling objects, defects, and damage caused by water or electrical malfunctions, depending on the type of policy purchased.

It is important to know what is and what is not covered by the policy. For example, the following are common exclusions from coverage:

- Loss caused by collapse of the structure due to faulty construction or geological shifts or earthquake (earthquake coverage can be purchased for an extra premium; it usually has a deduction of ten percent of the amount insured)
- Freezing, when the dwelling is vacant

- Vandalism, if the dwelling has been vacant for 30 or more days
- Constant or repeated water seepage
- Water damage, including flood, tidal wave or backed-up sewers (in some areas, flood insurance can be purchased that is subsidized by the Federal Government)
- Power failure
- Negligence or intentional damage caused by the insured
- War

Condominium insurance is a little different. The condominium complex will have insurance to protect the complex. That is part of what your condominium association dues pay for. However, since you are responsible for the interior of your unit, you will also need insurance to protect you. Also, you may want to insure against a cost assessment that the homeowner's association could charge against all unit owners to pay for damages not otherwise covered by the complex's insurance policy.

The personal property protection for the contents of your house will also be limited unless extra coverage is purchased. For example, a basic policy only covers the loss of up to $200 in money and $1,000 for losses due to theft of jewelry, watches, furs, or precious stones.

The liability section of the policy protects you against the costs of damages caused by your negligence, regardless of where the damage was caused. This portion of the policy, like an auto policy, also covers the cost of attorneys and court costs in the event you are sued. Like an auto policy, the liability section will define the maximum coverage allowed (e.g., $100,000).

The liability portion of the policy also contains *exclusions* that define the areas against which you will not be covered, including:

- Intentional misconduct
- Bodily injury
- Damage arising out of business activities or professional services
- Damage caused by the operation of a vehicle, a water craft or an aircraft
- Transmitting communicable disease

- Injuries covered by worker's compensation

Renter's Insurance

Renter's insurance is similar to homeowner's insurance, with the exception that it will not protect against destruction of the premises, which, is, of course, the responsibility of the landlord.

Life Insurance

The life insurance contract, in its essence, is very simple: A person's life is insured. If that person dies while the policy is in effect, those named in the policy as *beneficiaries* receive an amount of money specified in the insurance policy. The person who takes out the insurance policy (usually, but not necessarily, the insured), is the owner of the policy, who has the right to name beneficiaries, cancel the policy, and otherwise control its management.

Term-life insurance policies are those taken out for a specific time, usually a policy that can be renewed each year. If the insured dies while the policy is in effect, the benefits must be paid. If the contract lapses, it ceases to exist and no benefits will be paid if the formerly insured person dies.

Things get a little more complicated when life insurance is also used as an investment vehicle. These policies are known generically as whole-life or cash-value life insurance. The life insurance company charges a higher premium for cash-value policies than it does term life policies. The excess money, minus costs and commissions, is then invested by the life insurance company and the return accrues cash value. This cash value can be borrowed against and must be returned to the owner if the policy is cancelled.

Cash-value life insurance also has certain unique tax benefits:

The Value That Accrues Is Tax Deferred. If someone opens a bank savings account, the interest income that accrues is subject to income tax. This is also true of the increased value in cash value policies. However, while taxes must be paid each year on the bank interest, the tax is deferred on the accrued value of a life insurance policy until it is cashed in by the owner. Moreover, if a tax is due, the policyholder can deduct the price of the premiums from the cash value received, thereby reducing or eliminating the tax. Also, if policy benefits are paid due to the death of the insured, the cash value merges with the benefit and no tax is owed. (For example, if you are the insured in a $100,000 policy that has accrued a $10,000 cash value and you die, your beneficiaries only receive $100,000, not $110,000. Thus, no tax is due.)

Money Borrowed Against the Cash Value Is Not Taxed. This gives the owner a source of cash with no tax consequences. There may, however, be policy consequences. Borrowing against the cash value of the policy may affect the amount of the benefit, and if the money is not repaid, the policy may lapse.

Both term-life insurance and cash-value life insurance proceeds paid to beneficiaries are not subject to income taxes. They are also usually not subject to inheritance taxes unless the beneficiary is the dead person's estate.

This closes our discussion of personal insurance. There is much more to learn about individual policies than space permits. You should also reread the discussion in this book about arbitration and other forms of alternative dispute resolution since you may have to involve yourself in such procedures if you have a dispute with your company.

12

HIRING BUILDING CONTRACTORS

Tens of billions of dollars are spent each year by Americans on building contracts and home remodeling projects. Yet, few areas of consumerism cause more irritation or anxiety. In fact, the sad tales of homeowners having fits because they couldn't get a contractor to finish a job are so abundant they have almost become cliches.

This chapter will provide you with an overview of the ins and outs of working with a building contractor. We will discuss the importance of licensing, the concept of bonding and the difference between a general contractor and a subcontractor. We will give you some tips on retaining a contractor and we'll address the important concept of mechanic's liens and how they can impact the title to your property. Finally, we will discuss some strategies you can use to make sure that your building contract contains clauses to help ensure the job gets done on time and on budget.

LICENSED CONTRACTORS

The conduct of the business of those who work in the building trade is regulated by each state's laws. These laws can be quite complex and regulate a wide range of crafts. For example, painters, carpenters, plumbers, electricians, roofers and many others fall under the scope of state regulation. (For a complete list of trades that come under licensing requirements in your state, contact the State Licensing Board.)

Licensing

In order to legally contract with you to perform work in the building trade, a craftsperson must be licensed. The method of obtaining a license is established by law and usually requires a minimum amount of experience, education, training and the passing of a state test. The state agency in charge of licensing is usually called the Contractor's Licensing Board.

Bonding

In order to keep their license active, a building contractor must be bonded. A bond is money set aside by the contractor or a bonding company to guarantee performance and honesty, and to pay for damages that the contractor may cause should he or she be either unwilling or unable to pay.

The fact of bonding is less impressive than it may seem at first blush. That is because the required bonds are generally quite low, usually only a few thousand dollars. Moreover, the bond is to protect against all losses suffered by *all* the contractor's customers. Unfortunately, if a building contractor is unethical or incompetent, there will probably be many customers after a piece of his or her bank account. Needless to say, if there are 20 customers going after a $5,000 bond, the money will not go very far.

Insurance

Some people confuse bonding with insurance. Whenever there is a building job there is a chance that a worker is going to be hurt. Thus, while it may not be required by the state, a building contractor should have liability insurance and workers compensation insurance to pay for the cost of injuries that occur on your property. Otherwise, you may find that you or your homeowner's insurance may have to pay. At that point, other than complaining to licensing boards (which can take a license but not give you money) or seeking to sue the contractor (which may be pointless if the contractor has "skipped town" or gone broke), there may not be much that can be done to help you. For that reason, be *very careful* when selecting a contractor (see below).

General Contractors and Subcontractors

If your building job requires you to hire several different tradespeople— carpenter, plasterer, electrician, plumber, tiler, etc.— you are probably better off hiring a general contractor to do the work.

A general contractor has a special license that qualifies him or her to supervise an entire building project. The general contractor will hire and pay the workers, oversee their work and otherwise be responsible for the job being completed pursuant to the contract terms. Thus, the general contractor will have a wide range of knowledge about most or all of the building crafts that may be utilized in a building project. Using a general contractor also makes it easy on you since you will only have to interview and hire one person, not everyone who will work on your home. They are more likely than you to know the best subcontractors for a job. And, the general contractor will be legally responsible for the work conforming to your town or city's building codes. (Legally, you can perform the services of a general contractor. If you do, you will be known as an owner/ builder.)

A subcontractor is a craftsperson who works in the subareas of the building trade. If hired directly by you, you will have to negotiate the terms of the contract that the subcontractor will work under. If you use a general contractor, you will have no direct contact with a subcontractor and they will be answerable to, and paid by the general contractor, not you. (However, you could be forced to pay if the general skips out on that obligation. See the discussion of mechanic's liens.) We'll have more on the subcontractors and your responsibility to them later in the discussion of the building contract.

Architects

Many building projects are not large enough to require an architect. However, if you are planning a large construction project, such as building a house or adding a room, architects can offer you a variety of important services. Among them are:

- Conceiving the project based on what you want
- Preparing plans that will be followed by the builders
- Making sure the project is planned with efficiency and economy as important considerations
- Sorting out issues of what building materials to use and making sure the project conforms to regulations such as zoning laws and inspections
- Overseeing the general contractor

Architects, of course, get paid for their services, usually quite well, thereby adding to the cost of the job. Thus, the decision whether to employ an architect will depend on your budget, among other considerations.

THE BUILDING PROJECT

A building project takes place in several phases. Usually, the general contractor handles these issues, but if you plan on being an owner/builder, you need to know what will be happening:

Creating the Plans. Each building contract will refer to plans that the general contractor is to follow. These plans may be prepared by an architect, the general contractor may be responsible for obtaining them (depending on the terms of the building contract), or you may take your ideas to a draftsman who can prepare plans. The plans should contain job specifications and demonstrate that they comply with local building codes.

Obtain a Building Permit. You will need the permission of local government before beginning most jobs of any size or complexity. (This doesn't apply if you have something relatively simple done, like repaving your driveway.) The local government gives its permission to build according to the plans you have submitted by issuing a *building permit.* If you are using a general contractor, consider getting the permit in the contractor's name. In that way, the contractor may be held financially responsible for any corrections that must be made if the work does not pass inspection.

Do the Work. The work can begin after the building permit is received. You will want to be sure that all of the materials used and methods utilized will meet local building codes. Otherwise, the whole project may have to be torn down and redone.

Get an Inspection. In order for your construction job to be legally completed, it will require the approval of a building inspector, whose job it is to make sure the work was performed according to plans and applicable building codes. There may be several inspections required during the course of the project. If the inspector passes the job, it can go on to the next phase or be considered complete. If it does not, the work will have to be redone pursuant to the inspector's instructions.

For more information on the specific tasks you must perform under local building codes, contact your local office of building inspectors. The telephone number can be found in the local government section of your telephone book.

FINDING A GOOD CONTRACTOR

Since a building job is complicated, and with so much at stake in terms of emotional and financial investment, getting the right contractor may be the most important thing you do to ensure a satisfactory experience. Here are some tips:

Decide on the Kind of Contractor You Need

This isn't tough, if you have a specific job in mind. Thus, if you want to have your kitchen sink replaced, you will want a plumber. If you are rewiring your home, you will want an electrician. If you have a lot of different tasks involved, you will probably want a general contractor, unless you feel competent to act as an owner/builder.

Get Referrals

Just as finding the right lawyer and doctor is best performed through good referrals, so too is finding a good contractor. Here are some sources of information:

People You Know. If someone you know has had a good experience with a building contractor, you may want to interview that person.

Your Banker. If you are financing your building project (see below), your lender may have names of contractors that have a good reputation in the community and whom the lender has found have performed work on time and on budget.

A Real Estate Agent. Real estate agents also know the names of local builders. Be sure the agent is one you trust and that the referral is not based on a kickback scheme.

Your Homeowner's Insurance Agent. Insurance agents who deal with real property often know the names of building contractors with trustworthy reputations.

Other Contractors. If you don't need a general contractor but are looking for a good plumber, you may want to ask a general contractor you know for the names of people he or she uses. Or, if you need a general contractor and know other craftspersons, such as a plumber or electrician, ask them for some names of general contractors they know to be competent and honest.

Get Bids

You will want to get competitive *bids* from several different contractors. You may not decide to take the lowest bid, depending on the totality of the circumstances, but by getting competitive bids, you will know the general fair market value of the job you want done.

Research the Candidate

Before signing with any contractor, be sure to check his or her credentials and references. Here are some things to look for:

The Status of the License. Contact the Building Contractors Licensing Board and make sure your contractor's license is active and that the license is for the kind of work you are having done. Do not hire a contractor who is not licensed, since you cannot be sure they have the expertise to do the job, and there may be a reason they have not obtained a license. Moreover, if you hire an unlicensed person to do the work, the protections (such as they are) you have by using a licensed person (threat of government discipline, bond, etc.) will not exist.

The Status of the Bond. The contractor can tell you what bonding company issued the bond so that you can check it, or the Board of Contractors should be able to advise you if the bond is active.

References. Your contractor should have references from satisfied customers. Be sure to call several of these people, since phony names have been known to have been given as references by unscrupulous contractors.

Community Ties. Check into the ties between the contractor and the community: how long has he or she been in business, etc.

Be Sure the Contractor Has Insurance. For your own protection, your contractor should have liability and workers' compensation insurance. This should be part of the contract and made known when the job is offered for bidding. Otherwise, if someone is hurt on the job, you could be financially responsible.

Once you have compared contractors, what they want to charge and the date within which they expect to have the job completed, pick the contractor you believe offers the best chance of performing quality work at a reasonable price within a reasonable time. (In this regard, beware the deal that is "too good to be true." If one bid is substantially a better offer than the others, take the time to find out why.)

NEGOTIATING THE BUILDING CONTRACT

The success or failure of your building job will, in large part, be determined by the terms of the contract you negotiate. Here are some of the important issues to consider before signing:

What Is the Price?

Generally there are two types of payment plans that are acceptable for the consumer: cost-plus and flat fee.

Cost-Plus Fees. In a cost-plus deal, you agree to pay the contractor's out-of-pocket expenses (costs) plus an agreed upon percentage above that figure which represents the builder's profit.

Flat Fees. As the name implies, you agree to give the contractor a set fee for the work, and the contractor must supply all materials and expenses as well as earn a profit from the agreed-upon price.

Both kinds of pricing have their benefits and downsides. A fixed-price deal has the benefit of simplicity and predictability. However, there will be a financial incentive for the contractor to use cheaper materials and workers, since the less the contractor spends in expenses, the more that is kept as profit. A cost-plus deal is more flexible. You can change your mind about the type and quality of materials (which often happens) and not have to renegotiate the fee. You can also keep tabs on the actual cost of the materials and labor being used on the job. However, in a cost-plus job, the contractor may not have an incentive to keep costs down, since the higher the cost, the higher the "plus." (You may want to put an agreed-upon cap on costs in the cost-plus contract to protect you against a runaway price.)

How Are Payments to Be Made?

This is an important part of the contract. You do not want to pay all of the money up-front, but want to structure the payments, so that your contractor has an incentive to get the job done. This is best performed in the following manner:

Give a Small Down Payment. You will have to pay some money to get the job started. Try to make this as small as possible in the unlikely event that the contractor absconds with the payment and doesn't do the work. (If you get ripped off at this level, it is possible the bond will be able to repay you.)

Make Periodic Payments. You should create a payment schedule that lasts for the duration of the job. This is to give the contractor an incentive to keep working. Peg each payment to a significant job milestone, such as an inspection and approval, completion of plumbing, etc.

Put in a Retention Clause. A retention clause allows you to keep back a small percentage of each periodic payment, which you return when the job is completed in an appropriate manner. This helps you to keep the contractor's interest in correcting errors after the job is completed.

Final Payment. At the end of the job you will be asked to sign a completion certificate, a document that attests that the job has been completed to your satisfaction. Your contract should give you thirty days to sign this document and make final payment. During this time, you should inspect the work and make sure it is up to par, so that you can have corrections completed before you sign the certificate and make final payment. Otherwise, once paid, you might have difficulty getting the contractor to "squeeze you in" to correct mistakes.

Penalties. One of the biggest complaints consumers have is that contractors do not complete the job in a timely manner. To give your contractor an incentive to finish on time, be sure to include financial penalties for late performance.

Terms of Performance

The contract should specifically state what is to be done, the materials to be used and the time for performance. Also included should be the payment plan (discussed above) and how changes in the job are to be dealt with. In that regard, changes should always be in writing, in a document called a change order, so that if there is a later disagreement as to the terms of the changes, it will be set forth in black and white.

The Mechanic's Lien

By law, any building contractor and material supplier have the right to enforce payment through the use of a legal tool known as the *mechanic's lien.* A mechanic's lien allows a person who has worked on the property (or a material supplier) to make sure that you pay. If you do not pay as required under the contract, then the lien can be foreclosed and your property sold to pay off the debt. (Yes, in extreme cases, you can lose your house if a mechanic's lien is foreclosed.)

This can be a particular problem when using a general contractor. If a general contractor hires subcontractors and does not pay them, you will be responsible, *even though you have paid the general contractor.* That means, if the general contractor absconds with the funds, you must pay all unpaid subcontractors, or they can foreclose their mechanic's liens against your property.

There are some things you can do to protect yourself from such a nightmare:

Use a Fund Control Company. For a fee, a fund control company will make payments to the builder as the job progresses. You can provide that they are to inspect the work before payment is made. The fund control company will review disbursements made by the general contractor and the obtaining of necessary *releases* (a document subcontractors sign proving payment has been made and releasing the general contractor of any further liability). Thus, a fund control company can significantly reduce the risk of your suffering a mechanic's lien. (The company will, of course, charge a fee for this service. Be sure to explore this issue with the company before deciding to utilize the service. Also, sometimes lenders use a fund control company.)

Make Sure There Is Sufficient Bonding. If you want, you can require the contractor to qualify for and obtain a labor and materials bond and a performance bond. (This is in addition to the bond required by state law.) In this way, if the contractor fails to pay the subcontractors, the surety will have to. The contractor should pay for this as part of the contract. Of course, this will add modestly to the cost of the job.

Stay Involved With the Job. Make sure you receive copies of payments made to subcontractors and material suppliers and that all necessary releases have been signed. Also, try to be present when the work is being performed whenever possible, or have someone you trust checking on the work if you cannot be at home.

Right of Inspection

You should be sure to place in the contract your right to inspect the work being performed at any time.

Dispute Resolution

You can place requirements in the contract regarding dispute resolution. If alternative dispute resolution appeals to you, you can put in a mediation or arbitration clause.

By taking the time to negotiate a solid contract and by making sure the general contractor performs appropriately, you can go a long way toward assuring that your building project will be performed well and in a timely manner and that there will be no unpleasant surprises at the end of the job.

FINANCING THE JOB

If the building project is large, you may want to finance the job through a loan. There are several types of loans you may wish to consider:

The Construction Loan

A construction loan is a short loan, usually repayable within a year. The terms of the loan are generally more favorable then a conventional loan. Your compliance with repaying the loan will be assured by the lending institution being granted a lien on the property. Many construction loans have provisions, where, for a small additional cost, the construction loan can be converted into a conventional mortgage after construction is completed.

A Home Improvement Loan

Some banks and other lenders have special loans for home improvement. A home improvement loan is usually secured by a "second mortgage," or "equity line of credit," meaning that equity in your home secures the debt. If you don't pay, the mortgage can be foreclosed, even if you are up-to-date on your first mortgage payments. Second mortgages are generally due in a shorter period of time and there is usually a higher interest rate charged but the interest is tax-deductible.

Contractor Financing

Some contractors help their clients finance building projects. These loans may cost more, since the loan contract is often sold by the contractor to a finance company.

Government Assistance

If your project is to promote energy efficiency or structural renovation, you may qualify for a government grant or low-interest loan. For more information on assistance programs, go to your local library and ask the librarian to show you the Catalogue of Federal Public Assistance.

Different lenders offer different terms and charge different costs. Thus, be sure to shop around for the loan, just as you would for the contractor.

IF YOU HAVE A PROBLEM

Trouble shooting is an important part of your job as a consumer of building contractor services. It is the rare job that will not require some involvement on your part. If you stay organized and involved, you should be able to overcome most obstacles to satisfaction.

Talk to the Contractor

As with any consumer issue, your first step is to talk to the people involved. Don't be afraid to ask questions or complain if you are displeased. Also, be sure to point out problems sooner rather than later. There is a practical side to this advice. If your contractor breaches the contract, you have the right to sue for damages. However, you also have a responsibility. It is called the duty to mitigate damages. This means that you must take reasonable action to reduce the contractor's damages caused by his or her breach of contract. For example, let's say that you hire painters to paint the inside of your house. After they have painted one room, you notice that the paint being used is not the color you ordered. You say to yourself, "Ah, I know my rights. These painters are in breach of contract here. But I think I'll let them finish to see how this color looks. If I like it, fine. If I don't, I can always force them to repaint the house using the color I ordered."

There's only one problem with that approach: It won't work. You have a duty to keep the painter's damages as low as reasonably possible; you can't wait until the entire house has been painted and expect the contractor to redo the whole job. Should the matter ever go to court, you would only be entitled to damages equivalent to the cost of repainting one room, since that is all it would have cost the contractor if you had advised him or her of the mistake when you first discovered it.

Fire Your Contractor

If your contractor breaches the contract, you probably have the right to terminate the contract and bring someone else in to finish the job. (However, if the lapse is small, sometimes called a *minor breach*, this option will not be available, and your only recourse will be to recoup the damages caused by the deficient performance. For example, if the job is one week late being completed due to circumstances completely within the contractor's control, and you are staying at a hotel, the contractor may have to pay for the extra hotel bill.) Thus, before kicking a contractor off the job and hiring a new one to complete the job, discuss the matter with an attorney. Otherwise, you may end up paying twice (the money owed the original contractor under the contract and the money you paid the second contractor). Or, at the very least, you may end up fighting against an attempted foreclosure of a mechanic's lien.

Sue Your Contractor

If your contractor breaches the contract, you can sue for money damages. The measure of damages will generally be the expenses you incurred that were necessary to "make you whole;" that is, to obtain what you would have received had the contractor performed as promised. (Don't forget your duty to mitigate!) If the matter also involved fraud, you can also secure additional damages, such as for emotional distress or punitive damages.

Report Your Contractor

Just like a lawyer and doctor, if your contractor acts unethically, that fact can be reported to the authorities, who can thereafter take administrative action to suspend or revoke the contractor's license and/or require the contractor to reimburse you for damages.

Working with a building contractor need not cause your hair to turn gray or your blood pressure to rise. However, for things to go smoothly, you will have to be careful. This means, among other things, *putting everything in writing*, being home as much as possible when the work is being done, hiring only licensed people whom you have thoroughly checked out and paying only when you are satisfied with the work. Follow that course and you should be able to look back on the job with satisfaction.

PART 4

CREDIT &
DEALING WITH DEBT

13

CREDIT &
THE LAW

In this final text section of the book, we will discuss two very important areas of consumerism: the law of credit and dealing with debt. Both are inextricably linked. Most debt is created through loan transactions, generically known as credit. Likewise, most debt problems consumers face can find their genesis in consumers mistakenly over-using credit (which is easy to do considering how much credit is offered to consumers) or having so much debt that an unexpected financial setback, such as a job loss, sends them spinning toward insolvency.

In this chapter, we will describe the world of credit. We will describe some of the laws which govern credit, the ins and outs of a credit card agreement, the importance of the credit report, women and credit and what you can do if you are refused credit. We will also discuss the differences among different types of credit transactions. We will outline what you can do if you have a dispute with your credit card company or a business who accepted your credit card as the method of payment for services or products, and will conclude with a brief description of ways to avoid credit fraud.

THE KINDS OF CREDIT

In the last few decades, credit has become a way of American life. For example, before World War II, most consumer transactions were "cash and carry." Now, it is estimated that more than 70 percent of all families use credit cards in their everyday business affairs. Indeed, at last count, there were over 800 million credit cards in circulation. Then there are major purchases, such as a home, car, or furniture, which are accomplished with the help of credit. Truly, without credit, this country's economy would slow to a snail's pace, if not grind to a halt altogether.

Credit is, in actuality, another term for "loan." When you obtain credit, you have the right to borrow money, either at the time the credit is issued for a specific purpose, such as in a home loan, or at a later time, such as in a credit card.

There are two basic types of credit: open-ended lines of credit (credit cards) and closed-ended lines of credit (a car loan). But there are variations on these themes. For example, there are also secured lines of credit such as a mortgage and unsecured lines of credit, which is the opportunity to access credit based solely on a promise to repay.

Open-Ended Lines of Credit

If you are given a line of credit—that is, an amount you can borrow (but do not have to borrow)—then you have an open-ended line of credit. The most common form of open-ended credit is the credit card. For example, if you are issued a credit card with a credit limit of $5,000, you can borrow (use the credit card for purchases or cash advances) up to $5,000 without asking renewed permission from the lender (the credit card company).

Closed-Ended Lines of Credit

A closed-ended line of credit occurs when a specific amount of money is borrowed and repaid over a defined period of time. Typical examples of closed-ended lines of credit are auto loans and mortgages. If you later want more money, you will have to reapply.

Secured Versus Unsecured Lines of Credit

When you borrow money, you must pay it back (absent a special circumstance such as a bankruptcy) regardless of the type of credit you are using. (No news there.) However, the rights of your creditor if you fail to pay are different if the credit is secured than if the credit is unsecured.

When you obtain a secured line of credit, you pledge property as collateral, which serves as security protecting the lender's right to be repaid. (A security gives the lender an ownership interest in the property until the loan is repaid in full.) If the loan is not repaid, the property can be seized and sold to pay off the unpaid balance.

For example, if you borrow money to buy a car, the lender will probably insist on securing the loan with the car. This is done by the lender keeping possession of the pink slip (certificate of ownership) to the vehicle until the loan is paid in full and by having a clause in the loan contract permitting the lender to repossess the car if the loan is not paid. (The creditor will then auction off the car and apply the money received to your debt. Depending on your loan, you may or may not be responsible for the difference, if any.) By creating a security in property, the lender protects itself both against your failure to pay *and* preserves its rights to the secured property against other creditors who might otherwise be able to use the property to satisfy your debt to them. (See Chapter 14.)

An unsecured line of credit means that the lender does not have the right to repossess any property to satisfy the unpaid debt. If you don't pay an unsecured creditor, it must bring a lawsuit against you and obtain a court judgment stating that you owe the money. Then, and only then, can it seize your property and other assets to satisfy the debt. You may also have increased rights as a debtor against unsecured creditors, since their rights to seize property can be limited or the debt can be extinguished in bankruptcy. (A secured creditor can repossess the security despite a bankruptcy. See Chapter 14.)

Credit Cards

Perhaps the most common form of loan most consumers obtain is the credit card. A credit card is usually an open-ended, unsecured line of credit (although there are secured credit cards, guaranteed by money in a bank account, by investments or by equity in a house).

Your rights and obligations with regard to the credit card and the issuing company are listed in the credit card agreement. The credit card agreement is a contract that is enforceable in a court of law. Given the power of credit card companies, many of the terms of the agreement as well as your rights vis-à-vis credit card companies are regulated by law. Look for the following terms in your credit card agreement:

Your Maximum Credit Limit. This sets the upper limit of your open-ended line of credit.

The Interest Rate You Will Pay. If you don't pay the balance of a credit card upon receiving the bill, you will be charged interest. The credit agreement sets forth the amount you can be charged and how the interest is computed. For example, some credit agreements will compute interest on the average daily balance each month, while others compute the interest only after deducting all credits, such as payments and returns (called the adjustable monthly balance). The method of computing interest can be almost as important as the interest rate in determining the cost to you of the credit. (Many credit card companies charge exorbitant interest rates, greatly increasing the cost of credit for those who do not pay the entire monthly balance in full.)

Grace Period. Credit card agreements usually provide for grace periods, typically 20 days from the issuance of the credit statement, within which you can pay the bill in full without incurring any interest for the unpaid balance.

Membership Fee. Some credit cards charge a yearly fee, generally between $25-$50, for the privilege of having access to the line of credit. Others do not.

Late Fees. If you make a late payment, you will be charged a fee, typically $10–$15 by the company. The amount of late fee will be set forth in your credit agreement.

Minimum Payment. Many consumers do not pay their credit card balances in full each month. That is fine with the credit card company since they will earn interest on the money you have borrowed. (Credit card interest rates tend to be among the highest in the country.) However, you will be required to make at least a minimum payment on the balance. The method by which the credit card company determines the minimum payment will be set forth in the credit agreement.

Cash Advance Rights. Some agreements will restrict your use of the credit card to paying for goods and services. Others permit you to borrow cash (called a cash advance). The terms for borrowing cash usually include an additional fee for the advance, adding to the overall cost of the loan.

Perquisites. Some credit agreements also offer you special deals, such as extended warranty protections or frequent flyer mileage on an airline, each time you use the card.

There is a problem with credit card agreements that do not exist in most other forms of credit: The credit card company can unilaterally change the terms of the agreement. However, if the company intends to do so, it must give you at least 30 days advance notice. (This notice will usually come with your credit card statement.) All loans made prior to the effective date of the notice will usually come under the old terms. If you continue to use the credit card after the new terms go into effect, that will be deemed acceptance of the new terms.

YOUR CREDIT REPORT

Consumer credit is at an all-time high. Companies have set up a system to track people's credit lives in order to better determine to whom to grant or deny credit. This system is operated by companies known as *credit bureaus.* Credit bureaus keep computerized records of how much you have borrowed, your credit lines and your payment history, whether you have any court judgments against you and the like. Potential lenders have access to your credit report if you give your written permission. (If you want the credit then you will give your permission, since if you refuse, you will not receive a loan.) Existing creditors can access your credit report at any time.

If the credit bureau issues a report that the potential lender does not like, the lender may turn you down for credit. (The reporting agencies do not tell lenders whether to give loans. They supply the information that is relied upon by the lenders in part, in making its decision whether to extend credit.) If your request for a loan is turned down, you have rights under the law known as the Fair Credit Reporting Act, a federal law passed to help curb abuses in the reporting system. (Mistakes can destroy a person's creditworthiness.)

Under the Fair Credit Reporting Act, if you are turned down for credit because of information in your credit report, you have the right to the following:

To Know Which Credit Bureau Issued the Credit Report(s). That means you have the right to the name and address of the bureau and where you can write to receive a copy of your report.

You Have a Right to a Free Copy of the Report. In order to receive a free report, you must write the credit reporting company within 30 days of the turndown. (You can purchase a copy of your credit report at any time. Also, TRW, one of the nation's largest credit bureaus, allows you to have one free report per year. Mail your request to: TRW Box 2350, Chatsworth, CA 91313-2350.)

You Have the Right to Know Why Credit Was Declined. In its written refusal to issue you credit, the credit company has to list the specific reasons why you were refused credit.

You Have the Right to Dispute Information In Your Credit Report. If you look at a copy of your credit report and find what appears to be an error (not an unusual event), you have the right to dispute the information. This must be done in writing through a letter to the credit reporting company pointing out the mistake.

When you write such a letter, the credit reporting company is legally bound to check with the credit sources that you claim have issued a mistaken report. If it cannot verify the information, it must take the information off of the report. You also have the legal right to have corrected copies of your report sent to all credit companies or lenders which have requested a credit report on you during the previous six months. Some credit bureaus will also allow you to add a statement to your files explaining why you believe information is inaccurate. (That being said, many companies are maddeningly slow in complying with their legal obligations. However, unless you take action, no one will know the mistake has been made.)

Here is a sample letter:

Acme Credit Reporting Company
50 Blewit Square
Mistake, OK, 00000
Re: Credit Report Dated October 13, 1994

To Whom It May Concern:
On October 13, 1994, you company issued a credit report on me to Ajax Mastercard. I have enclosed a copy of this report.
This report contains erroneous information. Specifically, it contains the following mistakes:
1) I have never borrowed money from Usury Credit Corp. as the report states. Therefore, I can never have been late in making payments to that company.
2) I was late paying my account to Just Finance in April and May, 1992. The reason was that my home was destroyed in a fire and there was a period of time when my personal financial affairs were in a state of confusion. I did make up all late payments, and in fact, have paid that debt in full. Would you please reflect the cause for the late payment in the future?
Once you have investigated and verified the above, please notify all parties who have requested my credit report from you in the last six months and send me written proof that you have done so.

Very truly yours,

Your good credit is an important asset that can mean the difference between having access to goods and services and being forced to pay cash for every purchase. That being so, it is up to you to use the laws available to protect it.

CREDIT DISCRIMINATION

The Equal Credit Opportunity Act (ECOA)

The Equal Credit Opportunity Act (ECOA) is a federal law that prohibits discrimination in credit based on race, gender, marital status, age or national origin. This means that the only basis for denying credit must be an objective finding of credit unworthiness based on credit history, income and other such considerations. Among the legal benefits of the ECOA are the following:

It Gives Married Women a Credit History. Formerly, most credit records of married couples were kept in the name of the husband only. This meant that married women who got divorced, were widowed and/or who sought credit in their own names were often denied on the basis of having no credit history. Under the ECOA, credit grantors must now report credit history of joint accounts in both spouse's names, giving married women a credit history. However, if your spouse has a bad credit history, that could end up on your report if you obtained joint credit.

If You Apply For Credit In Your Own Name, You Usually Cannot Be Asked About Your Marital Status. However, if you live in a community property state (Arizona, California, Idaho, Louisiana, New Mexico, Nevada, Texas, and Washington), and your spouse will be using the account or will be partially or fully responsible for paying the account, this may not apply.

You Need Not Have Your Husband's Signature on the Credit Application. If you are a married woman applying for credit in your own name, you do not need your husband's consent or signature. If, however, you intend to use property owned jointly as a security, his signature will be required.

You Cannot Be Discouraged From Applying For Credit Based On Marital Status. This may be especially important for widows who used to complain they were told not to bother trying for credit since their husband had died.

A Creditor Cannot Take Your Race Into Account When Determining Whether to Grant Credit. Unfortunately, too many banks and other lenders seem to do so in a process known as "red lining." (Red lining is refusing to issue credit to people living in a defined area, usually because it is a place where minorities live.)

A Creditor Cannot Take Your Age Into Account When Determining Whether to Grant Credit. However, there are limited exceptions. For example, if you are about to retire, the creditor can take that into account.

If you suspect you have been discriminated against, here is what you should do:

- Complain to the creditor and let them know that they may have violated the law.
- Report violations to the Federal Trade Commission at Sixth Street and Pennsylvania Ave., N.W., Washington, DC 20580, telephone (202) 326-2000.
- Check with your state Attorney General's office to see if any state laws have been violated.
- If you are ambitious, you can bring a court action in Federal Court. If you are successful, you can recover any actual damages (money you lost because of the discrimination) be awarded a penalty, and receive compensation for attorney's fees. However, the damages you can receive may be limited, so be sure the "benefit" you might receive if you win is worth the "burden" in terms of costs and time of bringing the case to court.

CORRECTING BILLING ERRORS

Many people mistakenly believe that credit companies never make mistakes in their billing. This can be an expensive belief. Computers notwithstanding, mistakes happen, and you are the only one who will be there to catch them.

The Fair Credit Billing Act

This law gives consumers the right to correct mistakes on their credit card bills and has established the manner in which such mistakes are to be handled. That procedure is as follows:

- If you believe a mistake has been made, you must notify the creditor. That notification must be *in writing* and delivered within 60 days of the date the statement on which the charge appeared was sent to you. Telephone complaints do not legally protect your rights.
- The credit card or loan company then must acknowledge the letter of complaint within 30 days.
- While waiting for a reply from the credit card company, you do not have to pay the amount in dispute. However, you do have to pay amounts that are not in dispute.
- Your creditor has two billing periods, or 90 days, whichever comes first, to resolve the matter. If the company does not follow the law in resolving the complaint, it may be required to forfeit the first $50 of the charge, even if the original bill was not in error.
- If the credit card company determines you're wrong and you then do not pay promptly, it can report delinquent payments to credit bureaus.

WITHHOLDING PAYMENTS TO RETAILERS

If there's a problem with merchandise paid for by credit card, you may be able to withhold payment until the matter is resolved, thanks to the Truth-in-Lending Act. This federal law gives consumers important leverage. If a consumer receives defective merchandise or improper services purchased by credit card, *payment can be withheld* to the credit card company, so long as the consumer makes a good-faith effort to resolve the matter directly with the merchant (who, otherwise, will not be paid by the credit card company.)

Unfortunately, the right does not apply in every situation. In order for the right to apply, the goods purchased must exceed $50 in value and the sale must have taken place within 100 miles of your current address.

To take advantage of this law, you must inform the credit card company in writing that the merchandise is defective and that you do not want them to pay the merchant. In such cases, the matter will be treated as a billing error (see above). Because the law requires you to make a good-faith effort to resolve the matter directly with the merchant, be sure to make complaints to the merchant in writing so that you can prove your "good faith."

AVOIDING CREDIT CARD FRAUD

Unauthorized use of credit cards is a significant problem in the United States. You too can be victimized if you are not careful. Here are some tips that can keep unauthorized others from learning your credit card number or from having your $10 purchase converted into a $100 purchase:

- Report your lost or stolen cards immediately
- Always tear up carbons
- Be sure the totals for your purchase are written in ink
- Don't allow merchants to write your credit card number on a check
- Don't give your credit card number over the telephone unless you are very sure you are dealing with a reputable company or organization
- If you receive a personalized "pre-approved" credit card offer, tear it up if you do not intend to accept the offer
- Don't let unauthorized people have access to your social security number
- Verify charges against receipts when you receive your statements

If someone uses your card without authorization, the law limits your personal liability to $50 for each card until you report the theft, loss or unauthorized use. After you report the problem, you are not responsible for the charges.

There are many other issues involving credit and credit card usage: How do you get a lower interest rate? What is the best way to manage credit? Are there any credit cards that don't have annual fees? These questions and more can be answered by the nonprofit organization Bankcard Holders of America, an activist and educational association for credit card consumers. For more information, contact:

Bankcard Holders of America
560 Herndon Parkway, Ste. 120
Herndon, VA 22070
(703) 481-1110

14

DEBTOR'S
RIGHTS

Most Americans accumulate significant debt from credit cards, mortgages, school loans, car loans and other types of loans. If you are having difficulty managing your debt, there are some options you might want to consider, including bankruptcy.

You should also know that there is a federal law, called the Fair Debt Collection Practices Act, that protects you from the extreme collection tactics some creditors will try to use.

This chapter will discuss the various ways you can seek to manage your debt, your rights vis-à-vis collection agencies, and the law of bankruptcy, including its consequences.

HOW TO TELL YOUR DEBT IS OUT OF CONTROL

Here are some danger signals that your debt may be getting out of hand:

You Only Pay the Minimum Amount Each Month. Minimum payments are seductive. They allow you to temporarily enjoy a higher standard of living than your income permits by allowing you to buy more on credit each month than you pay with the small minimum payment.

But sooner or later the chickens come home to roost. Eventually, if you charge enough, you will hit your maximum and can charge no further. Unfortunately, what many people do at that point is get another credit card (many companies issue credit far beyond people's ability to pay it back) and start the process again. Eventually, several cards are "maxed out," and the consumer is so deeply in debt the light at the end of the tunnel can't even be seen.

You've Reached Your Credit Limit on Several Cards. See above.

Your Debt Keeps You From Saving Money. If you can't stash any of your money away for savings because you have so many bill payments, you are probably too deeply in debt.

You Use Debt to Pay Debt. Borrowing to pay debt will eventually lead you to the precipice of bankruptcy.

You're Chronically Late Making Payments. This is a good sign your debt is going out of control.

You're Frequently Pursued By Debt Collectors. You are probably already experiencing a financial meltdown.

GET SOME HELP

If you find yourself in financial trouble, you have some options, including bankruptcy.

Self Help

There are many things you can do to get financial help. Here are some tips:

Cut Back Your Spending. For many, this may not be an option. But for most of us, there are discretionary spending habits we can cut out. For example, going out to dinner at fancy restaurants and saying "charge it;" buying clothes or other purchases on impulse; taking vacations; in general, spending for other than necessities.

Cancel Your Credit Cards. If you are not already maxed out on all your credit cards, cancel them. (Act quickly while your willpower is strong.) If you must, keep a card for emergencies, but be sure that is all it is reserved for.

Make Higher Payments. The more you pay in payments, the quicker you will be out of debt. If you can't afford higher payments, maintain minimum payments because a little principal will be paid each month, along with all of the interest you are paying.

Put Yourself On a Budget. Get out some paper and your calculator. List your debts, your monthly payments and your income. See how much you are spending and find places to cut down. Then, create a bare-bones budget. Any surplus left over from your income should be used to pay down debt, or should be saved, or a little of both. If your budget shows you can get your debt down, then you can probably get out of debt by yourself. But you must stick to your budget.

Make Arrangements With Your Creditors. If you are sinking beneath the waves, your creditors may be willing to accommodate you by accepting lower monthly payments, suspending interest or taking a lump-sum payment as payment in full even though it is less than you actually owe.

Be Patient. It probably took years for you to get into this mess and it may take as long to get out. Just take it one day at a time. If you slip, don't say to heck with it, but to quote the famous song, "pick yourself up, dust yourself off and start all over again."

Get Help

If you are unable to handle the matter on your own, or if your creditors won't give you a break, you should call in outside help.

The best place to go is probably your local branch of *Consumer Credit Counselor Services* (CCCS). CCCS is a nonprofit organization, financed by credit card companies and other business interests that can help you in many significant ways:

Teach You to Better Manage Your Money. The counselors will help you prepare a budget and give you tips on money management.

Set Up a Debt Management Plan. The CCCS is best known for helping people set up what they call the Debt Management Plan (DMP).

The DMP is a structured recovery plan that "forces" you to be responsible. Here's how it works:

- CCCS contacts your creditors and works out a special arrangement, such as lower payments, suspension of interest and the like. (Most creditors will cooperate since failure to do so may lead you to seek bankruptcy protection.) Debtors are also asked to defer lawsuits or other collection actions against you.
- The CCCS helps you devise a budget and collects a monthly payment from you to disperse to your creditors. In that way, you are provided with an organized, stress-free way of handling repayment of your debt.
- You are prohibited from incurring new debt. If you do so, you are out of the program.
- In two or three years, you are back on your feet. By spreading the pain over a period of time and making special deals, you may be able to get out of the hole much sooner and cheaper than you would on your own.

CCCS cannot guarantee that creditors will cooperate and they cannot stop a creditor from pursuing you in court, nor can they improve your credit rating, but they can bring discipline to an undisciplined situation, giving you the breathing room you need to enjoy life as you dig yourself out of debt.

To find the nearest CCCS office, call their toll-free referral line at (800) 388-CCCS.

If this doesn't work for you, you may want to try private accountants and get advice about possibly filing bankruptcy.

BANKRUPTCY

Bankruptcy is intended to erase most, if not all of your debt and thereby give you another chance at life. It can also delay repossession of your car and the foreclosure of your house, allowing you extra time to make up back payments. And while a bankruptcy cannot prevent repossession of property used to secure a debt, it may be able to lower the payments on that debt. Bankruptcy can also restore utility service or prevent it from being cut off and stop wage garnishments and other such collection activities. However, a bankruptcy cannot protect a co-signer against having to pay the debt, even though the bankruptcy may relieve *you* of that obligation.

The Kinds of Bankruptcy

There are several types of bankruptcy, but we will focus only on those bankruptcies available to individual consumers (as opposed to businesses).

Chapter 7 Bankruptcy

Chapter 7 bankruptcy is known as liquidation bankruptcy. This is the bankruptcy most individuals pursue. It is designed to liquidate your estate, allowing you to keep certain property, paying any money available to creditors and then wiping out all "dischargeable debts."

All property that you own can be sold by the court trustee in a bankruptcy, unless it is exempted by state law. (Bankruptcy takes place in Federal Bankruptcy Court, but state laws regarding exemptions applies.) Exempted property may include equity in your house, your car, tools of business, etc. To find out what property is exempt from liquidation, contact a neighborhood or law school legal clinic, a bankruptcy lawyer or research the issue in a law library.

Dischargeable debts generally include the following:

- Credit card debts

- Other unsecured debts, such as for medical bills
- Court judgments for civil wrongs such as negligence or breach of contract
- Utility arrears
- Some tax payments

Nondischargeable debts generally include the following:

- Alimony and child support arrears
- Income taxes
- Civil judgments for intentional torts, such as fraud
- Debts incurred after the bankruptcy has been filed
- Debts that, if discharged, would constitute a fraud (for example, if you know you are going bankrupt and go out and buy a houseful of furniture on credit)
- Debts not listed on your Petition for Bankruptcy
- Student loans
- Debts incurred due to driving while intoxicated
- Fines and penalties owed to government agencies

A Chapter 7 Bankruptcy generally proceeds as follows:

You file a Petition for Bankruptcy (or have an attorney do it for you). Be sure to fill out the petition completely. Any debts you omit will not be discharged. You will have to pay a moderate filing fee, currently $120. If you have not hired an attorney, the court may allow you to pay the filing fee in payments.

Once the Petition is filed, there is an automatic stay which stops any actions being taken by creditors against you. The court clerk will notify your creditors but, if any collection efforts are made, be sure to let the creditor know about the filing.

A trustee will then be appointed by the court, who will represent the interests of unsecured creditors.

Shortly thereafter, you will have to appear in court at a proceeding known as the first meeting of creditors. There, your creditors have a right to examine your affairs, but they rarely appear. However, the trustee will ask you questions about your finances or the information you supplied with the Petition for Bankruptcy.

At that point, creditors can object to your claims of exemption or the dischargeability of the debt. If you have assets that can be liquidated, the trustee will do so. If there are claims that debts are not dischargeable, a hearing may be held to determine the merits of the assertion.

Finally, you will receive a Notice of Discharge. At that point, you no longer owe the money for all listed, dischargeable debts.

Chapter 13 Bankruptcy

Chapter 13 bankruptcies are also known as reorganization bankruptcies. (Family farmers act under Chapter 12. Chapter 13 is similar in some ways to business reorganizations under Chapter 11.) A reorganization is designed to buy you time to pay off creditors, including secured debts such as mortgages and car payments.

The advantage of a Chapter 13 bankruptcy is that your property will not be liquidated. You will make payments to a *trustee* over a three-year period, based on a plan of reorganization that you submit that is accepted by the court. (Reorganization can go as long as five years with court approval.)

Once you have completed your payments, you will receive a discharge, just as in a Chapter 7 bankruptcy. Also, some debts not dischargeable in Chapter 7 may be discharged in Chapter 13 (since payments will have been made on them). Chapter 13 can reduce payments and even principal amounts owed to your creditors.

The Impact of Bankruptcy

Bankruptcy will have a major effect on your future. There are both advantages and disadvantages. Here is an overview:

Pros. There are several benefits you will receive from a bankruptcy:

- Discharge from most debts
- Keeping some of your property, such as your car
- Leverage in dealing with secured creditors
- Protection against wage garnishments or other enforcement of judgments
- Stays of foreclosures and evictions

Cons. There are some downsides to bankruptcy as well, including:

- Loss of non-exempt property
- Credit record will reflect bankruptcy for 10 years (many creditors will not loan money to someone who has gone through bankruptcy)
- Emotions about filing for bankruptcy

As can be seen from the above discussion, bankruptcy is serious, so you should consult with an attorney at a legal clinic or bankruptcy firm, before deciding whether or not to do it.

There is an excellent book that provides more information on dealing with debt than could be provided here. It is called *Surviving Debt: Counseling Families in Financial Trouble,* written and published by the National Consumer Law Center. The book can be found at your local bookstore (perhaps by special order) or obtained directly by contacting:

The National Consumer Law Center
11 Beacon Street
Boston, MA 02108
(617) 523-8010

YOUR RIGHTS AGAINST COLLECTION AGENCIES

Collection agencies are businesses that buy bad debt from credit card companies, banks and other creditors and then seek to collect it. Generally, the collection agency keeps a large percentage of what they collect, returning the rest to the original creditor. Since they essentially work on contingency, and make no money unless they actually collect owed money, they are quite aggressive in trying to get debtors to pay.

Because many collection agencies did not know the difference between aggressive collection and harassment, the Fair Debt Collection Practices Act was passed to protect debtors from improper collection activities. Here are some of the law's most important provisions:

- Collectors are permitted to contact you in person, by mail, telephone or telegram. However, you may not be contacted at unusual times or places, such as before 8:00 A.M. or after 9:00 P.M. Unless you say otherwise, your collectors cannot contact you at work.
- If you do not wish to be contacted by telephone, you can direct the collectors by mail to stop doing so. At that point, the telephone calls and letters have to stop, other than a notice of action they intend to take.
- Collectors cannot harass you. They cannot threaten you with violence or public embarrassment. They cannot use profane language, or make repeated telephone calls with the purpose of causing you emotional distress. They cannot call your neighbors, co-workers, family or boss about your debt.
- Collectors cannot make false statements to you. They cannot falsely represent they are a government agency, an attorney (unless the collector is an attorney) or misrepresent the amount of your debt. They cannot tell you that you will be arrested for debt. (There are no such things as debtors' prisons anymore.)
- Collectors cannot engage in unfair practices, such as depositing a post-dated check before the date on the check, take property other than through legal means (such as garnishment after a judgment), or contact you by post card or by mail in such a way that a casual reader could tell the communication is from a collection agency.

(Your state will also have laws governing the activities of collection agencies.)

If the debt collector breaks the law, you can sue or bring an administrative complaint against the collection agency. To make a complaint, write to:

The Federal Trade Commission
Bureau of Consumer Protection
Division of Credit Practices
6th St. and Pennsylvania Ave., N.W.
Washington, DC 20580
(202) 326-2000

APPENDICES

STATE BAR PROGRAMS FOR RESOLVING COMPLAINTS AGAINST LAWYERS

This appendix lists addresses and phone numbers for grievance committees, *Client Security Fund* offices and fee arbitration programs for all 50 states, the District of Columbia, the Virgin Islands and Puerto Rico.

Where state offices handle the matter, that office is listed. If the issue is handled at a local office, that office is either listed or we suggest you contact the state office for a local referral.

Data on grievance committees and *Client Security Fund* offices were compiled by the American Bar Association. Fee arbitration program data were compiled by HALT. Because the names and addresses of state agencies may change at any time, you should verify the information with your state bar or the American Bar Association.

ALABAMA
Attorney Grievance
State Office:
General Counsel
Alabama State Bar
Center for Professional
   Responsibility
415 Dexter Ave.
Montgomery, AL 36101
(205) 269-1515

Client Security Fund
Executive Director
Alabama State Bar
P.O. Box 671
415 Dexter Ave.
Montgomery, AL 36101
(205) 269-1515

Fee Arbitration
No statewide program, state bar
   refers cases to local Fee Arbitration where available. (Address,
   telephone same as Client
   Security Fund.)

ALASKA
Attorney Grievance
State Office:
Bar Counsel
Alaska Bar Assn.
P.O. Box 100279
Anchorage, AK 99510-0279
(907) 272-7469

Client Security Fund
Asst. Bar Counsel
(Address, telephone same as
   Attorney Grievance.)

Fee Arbitration
Fee Arbitration Committee
(Address, telephone same as
    Attorney Grievance.)

ARIZONA
Attorney Grievance
State Office:
Chief Bar Counsel
State Bar of Arizona
363 N. First Ave.
Phoenix, AZ 85003-1580
(602) 252-4804; Ext. 225

Client Security Fund
Special Services Counsel
(Address, telephone same as
Attorney Grievance.)

Fee Arbitration
Committee on Arbitration of Fee
    Disputes
(Address, telephone same as
Attorney Grievance.)

ARKANSAS
Attorney Grievance
State Office:
Supreme Court of Arkansas
Committee on Professional
    Conduct
364 Prospect Bldg.
1501 N. University
Little Rock, AR 72207
(501) 664-8658

Client Security Fund
Clerk
Arkansas Supreme Court Justice
    Bldg.
625 Marshall St.
Little Rock, AR 72201
(501) 682-6849

Fee Arbitration
None.

CALIFORNIA
Attorney Grievance
Chief Trial Counsel
Intake/Legal Advice
State Bar of California
333 S. Beaudry Ave., 9th Fl.
Los Angeles, CA 90017-1466
(213) 580-5000
(800) 843-9053 (Calif. residents
    only)

Client Security Fund
(Address same as for
Attorney Grievance.)
(213) 580-5140
(800) 843-9053 (Calif. residents
    only)

Fee Arbitration
State Bar of California
Mandatory Fee Arbitration
100 Van Ness Ave., 28th Fl.
San Francisco, CA 94102-5238
(415) 241-2020

COLORADO
Attorney Grievance
State Office:
Disciplinary Counsel
Supreme Court of Colorado
600 17th St., Ste. 510 S.
Dominion Plaza Bldg.
Denver, CO 80202-5435
(303) 893-8121

Client Security Fund
Executive Director
Colorado Bar Assn.
1900 Grant St., Ste. 950
Denver, CO 80203-4309
(303) 860-1112

Fee Arbitration
Legal Fee Arbitration Committee
(Address, telephone same as
Client Security Fund.)

CONNECTICUT
Attorney Grievance
State Office:
Statewide Grievance Committee
287 Main St.
E. Hartford, CT 06118-1885
(203) 566-4163

Client Security Fund
Asst. Executive Director
Connecticut Bar Assn.
101 Corporate Place
Rocky Hill, CT 06067
(203) 721-0025

Fee Arbitration
Committee on Arbitration of Fee
    Disputes
(Address, telephone same as
Client Security Fund.)

DELAWARE
Attorney Grievance
State Office:
Disciplinary Counsel
Board on Professional
    Responsibility of the Supreme
    Court of Delaware
831 Tatnall St.
P.O. Box 1808
Wilmington, DE 19899
(302) 571-8703

Client Security Fund
Administrator
Delaware State Bar Assn.
1225 King St.
Wilmington, DE 19801
(302) 658-5279

Fee Arbitration
Fee Dispute Conciliation and
    Mediation Committee
(Address, telephone same as
Client Security Fund.)

DISTRICT OF COLUMBIA
Attorney Grievance
District Office:
Bar Counsel
District of Columbia Bar
Bldg. A, Rm. 127
515 5th St. NW
Washington, DC 20001-2797
(202) 638-1501

Client Security Fund
Asst. Executive Director
District of Columbia Bar
1250 H St., 6th Fl.
Washington, DC 20005-3908
(202) 737-4700

Fee Arbitration
Attorney-Client Arbitration Board
(Address, telephone same as
Client Security Fund.)

FLORIDA
Attorney Grievance
State Office:
Staff Counsel
Florida Bar
650 Apalachee Pkwy.
Tallahassee, FL 32399-2300
(800) 874-0005 (out-of-state)
(800) 342-8060 (FL residents only)
(904) 561-5600

Client Security Fund
Programs Division
(Address same as
Attorney Grievance.)
(904) 561-5600

Fee Arbitration
Fee Arbitration Committee
(Address, telephone same as
Attorney Grievance.)

GEORGIA
Attorney Grievance
State Office:
General Counsel
State Bar of Georgia
50 Hurt Plaza, Ste. 800
Atlanta, GA 30303-2934
(404) 527-8720

Client Security Fund
Asst. General Counsel
(Address, telephone same as
Attorney Grievance.)

Fee Arbitration
Committee on Arbitration of
Fee Disputes
(Address same as for Attorney
Grievance.)
(404) 527-8720

HAWAII
Attorney Grievance
State Office:
Chief Disciplinary Counsel
Office of Disciplinary Counsel
Supreme Court of the State of
    Hawaii
1164 Bishop St., Ste. 600
Honolulu, HI 96813
(808) 521-4591

Client Security Fund
Lawyers' Fund for Client Protection
c/o Office of the Chief Clerk
The Supreme Court of the State of
    Hawaii
P.O. Box 2560
Honolulu, HI 96804
(808) 599-8938

Fee Arbitration
Attorney-Client Coordination
    Committee
Hawaii State Bar Assn.
P.O. Box 26
Honolulu, HI 96810
(808) 537-1868

IDAHO
Attorney Grievance
State Office:
Bar Counsel
Idaho State Bar
P.O. Box 895
204 W. State St.
Boise, ID 83701-0895
(208) 342-8956

Client Security Fund
Executive Director
(Address, telephone same as
Attorney Grievance.)

Fee Arbitration
Fee Arbitration Program
(Address, telephone same as
Attorney Grievance.)

ILLINOIS
Attorney Grievance
Chicago and Northern Illinois:
Attorney Registration &
    Disciplinary Commission of the
    Supreme Court of Illinois
1 Prudential Plaza, Stes. 1100 &
    1500
130 E. Randolph Dr.
Chicago, IL 60601
(312) 565-2600

Central and Southern Illinois:
Illinois State Bar Assn.
Illinois Bar Center
424 S. 2nd St.
Springfield, IL 62701-1779
(217) 525-1760

Client Security Fund
Clients' Security Fund of the Bar of
  Illinois
Illinois Bar Center
424 S. 2nd St.
Springfield, IL   62701
(217) 525-1670

Fee Arbitration
Voluntary Fee Arbitration
(Address, telephone same as
Client Security Fund.)

INDIANA
Attorney Grievance
State Office:
Executive Secretary
Disciplinary Commission of the
  Supreme Court of Indiana
150 W. Market St., Rm. 628
Indianapolis, IN 46204
(317) 232-1807

Client Security Fund
Executive Director
Indiana Bar Center
Indiana State Bar Assn.
230 E. Ohio St.,
Indianapolis, IN 46204
(317) 639-5465

Fee Arbitration
No statewide program, state bar
  refers cases to local Fee
  Arbitration where available.
(Address, telephone same as
Client Security Fund.)

IOWA
Attorney Grievance
State Office:
Committee on Professional Ethics
  & Conduct

Iowa State Bar Assn.
521E. Locust St.
Des Moines, IA 50309-1911
(515) 243-3179

Client Security Fund
Asst. Court Administrator
Clients' Security Trust Fund
State Capitol
Des Moines, IA 50319
(515) 246-8076

Fee Arbitration
No statewide program, state bar
  refers cases to local Fee
  Arbitration where available.
(Address, telephone same as
Attorney Grievance.)

KANSAS
Attorney Grievance
State Office:
Disciplinary Administrator
Supreme Court of Kansas
Kansas Judicial Center, Rm. 278
301 W. 10th St.
Topeka, KS 66612
(913) 296-2486

Client Security Fund
Kansas State Bar Assn.
1200 Harrison St.
P.O. Box 1037
Topeka, KS 66601
(913) 234-5696

Fee Arbitration
No statewide program, state bar
  refers cases to local Fee
  Arbitration where available.
(Address, telephone same as
Attorney Grievance.)

KENTUCKY
Attorney Grievance
State Office:
Bar Counsel
Kentucky Bar Assn.
Kentucky Bar Center
514 W. Main St.
Frankfort, KY 40601-1883
(502) 564-3795

Client Security Fund
(Address, telephone same as
Attorney Grievance.)

Fee Arbitration
Legal Fee Arbitration Plan
(Address, telephone same as
Attorney Grievance.)

LOUISIANA
Attorney Grievance
State Office:
Office of the Disciplinary Counsel
Louisiana State Bar Assn.
601 St. Charles Ave., 4th Fl.
New Orleans, LA 70130
(504) 523-1414

Client Security Fund
Executive Counsel
(504) 566-1600
(Address, same as Attorney
    Grievance.)

Fee Arbitration
None.

MAINE
Attorney Grievance
State Office:
Bar Counsel
Maine Board of Overseers of the
    Bar
P.O. Box 1820
Augusta, ME 04332-1820
(207) 623-1121

Client Security Fund
(Address, telephone same as
Attorney Grievance.)

Fee Arbitration
Fee Arbitration Commission
(Address, telephone same as
Attorney Grievance.)

MARYLAND
Attorney Grievance
State Office:
Bar Counsel
Attorney Grievance Commission of
    Maryland
100 Community Pl., Ste. 3301
Crownsville, MD 21032-2027
(410) 514-7051

Client Security Fund
Administrator
208 Calvert St.
Salisbury, MD 21801
(301) 543-8410

Fee Arbitration
Committee on Resolution of Fee
    Disputes
(Address, telephone same as
Client Security Fund.)

MASSACHUSETTS
Attorney Grievance
State Office:
Bar Counsel
Massachusetts Board of Bar
    Overseers
75 Federal St., 7th Fl.
Boston, MA 02110
(617) 357-1860

Client Security Fund
Assistant Board Counsel
75 Federal St.
Boston, MA 02110
(617) 357-1860; Ext. 51

Fee Arbitration
Fee Arbitration Board
Massachusetts Bar Assn.
20 West St.
Boston, MA 02111
(617) 542-3602

MICHIGAN
Attorney Grievance
State Office:
Acting Grievance Administrator
Michigan Attorney Grievance
  Commission
Marquette Bldg., Ste. 256
243 W. Congress
Detroit, MI 48226
(313) 961-6585

Client Security Fund
State Bar of Michigan
306 Townsend St.
Lansing, MI 48933-2083
(517) 372-9030, ext. 3010

Fee Arbitration
Fee Arbitration Program
(Address, telephone same as
Attorney Grievance.)

MINNESOTA
Attorney Grievance
Director
Minnesota Office of Professional
  Responsibility
520 Lafayette Rd., Ste. 100
St. Paul, MN 55155-4196
(612) 296-3952
(800) 657-3601

Client Security Fund
Director
(Address, telephone same as
Attorney Grievance.)

Fee Arbitration
No statewide program, disciplinary
  committee refers cases to local
  Fee Arbitration where available.
(Address, telephone same as
Attorney Grievance.)

MISSISSIPPI
Attorney Grievance
State Office:
General Counsel
Mississippi State Bar
643 N. State St.
P.O. Box 2168
Jackson, MS 39225-2168
(601) 948-4471

Client Security Fund
Asst. General Counsel
(Address, telephone same as
Attorney Grievance.)

Fee Arbitration
Resolution of Fee Disputes
  Committee
(Address, telephone same as
Attorney Grievance.)

MISSOURI
Attorney Grievance
State Office:
General Chair
Missouri Supreme Court
Office of Chief Disciplinary
  Counsel
3335 America Ave.
Jefferson City, MO 65109
(314) 635-7400

Client Security Fund
Director of Programs
Missouri Bar
P.O. Box 119
Jefferson City, MO 65102
(314) 635-4128

Fee Arbitration
No statewide program, state bar
refers cases to local Fee Arbitra-
tion where available.
(Address, telephone same as
Attorney Grievance.)

MONTANA
Attorney Grievance
State Office:
Administrative Secretary
Commission on Practice of the
Supreme Court of Montana
Justice Bldg., Rm. 315
215 N. Sanders
Helena, MT 59620
(406) 444-2608

Client Security Fund
Executive Director
State Bar of Montana
P.O. Box 577
Helena, MT 59624
(406) 442-7660

Fee Arbitration
Voluntary Fee Arbitration
(Address, telephone same as
Client Security Fund.)

NEBRASKA
Attorney Grievance
State Office:
Counsel for Discipline
Nebraska State Bar Assn.
P.O. Box 81809
Lincoln, NE 68501
(402) 475-7091

Client Security Fund
Executive Director
Nebraska State Bar Assn.
635 S. 14th St.
Lincoln, NE 68508
(402) 475-7091

Fee Arbitration
None.

NEVADA
Attorney Grievance
State Office:
Bar Counsel
State Bar of Nevada
201 Las Vegas Blvd., South, Ste. 200
Las Vegas, NV 89101
(702) 382-2200

Client Security Fund
(Address, telephone same as
Attorney Grievance.)

Fee Arbitration
Voluntary Fee Arbitration Program
(Address, telephone same as
Attorney Grievance)

NEW HAMPSHIRE
Attorney Grievance
State Office:
Administrator
New Hampshire Supreme Court
Professional Conduct Committee
4 Park St., Ste. 304
Concord, NH 03301
(603) 224-5828

Client Security Fund
Staff Liason
Clients' Indemnity Fund
New Hampshire Bar Assn.
112 Pleasant St.
Concord, NH 03301
(603) 224-6942

Fee Arbitration
Fee Dispute Resolution Committee
(Address, telephone same as
Client Security Fund.)

NEW JERSEY

Attorney Grievance
State Office:
Director, Office of Attorney Ethics
Supreme Court of New Jersey
Richard J. Hughes Justice Complex,
  CN-963
25 W. Market St.
Trenton, NJ 08625
(609) 292-8750

Client Security Fund
Director and Counsel
(Address same as
Attorney Grievance, except
  CN-961)
(609) 984-7179

Fee Arbitration
District Fee Arbitration Committee
(Address, telephone same as
Attorney Grievance.)

NEW MEXICO

Attorney Grievance
State Office:
Chief Disciplinary Counsel
Disciplinary Board of the Supreme
  Court of New Mexico
400 Gold SW, Ste. 1100
Albuquerque, NM 87102
(505) 842-5781

Client Security Fund
State Bar of New Mexico
P.O. Box 25883
Albuquerque, NM 87125
(505) 842-6132

Fee Arbitration
Fee Arbitration Committee
State Bar of New Mexico
P.O. Box 25883
Albuquerque, NM 87125
(505) 842-6132

NEW YORK

Attorney Grievance
In New York City: (First Dept.:
  Bronx County)
Chief Counsel
Departmental Disciplinary Commit-
  tee for the First Judicial Dept.
41 Madison Ave., 39th Fl.
New York, NY 10010
(212) 685-1000

In New York City: (Second Dept.:
  Kings, Queens, Richmond
  Counties)
Chief Counsel
State of New York Grievance
  Committee for the 2nd and 11th
  Judicial Districts
Municipal Bldg., 12th Fl.
210 Joralemon St.
Brooklyn, NY 11201
(718) 624-7851

In New York State: (Second Dept.)
Chief Counsel
Grievance Committee for the 9th
  Judicial District
Crosswest Office Center
399 Knollwood Rd., Ste. 200
White Plains, NY 10603
(914) 949-4540

In New York State: (Second Dept.:
  Nassau, Suffolk Counties)
Chief Counsel
New York State Grievance Commit-
  tee for the 10th Judicial District
900 Ellison Ave., Rm. 304
Westbury, NY 11590
(516) 832-8585

In New York State: (Third Dept.)
Chief Attorney
3rd Department Committee on
  Professional Standards

Alfred E. Smith State Office Bldg.,
22nd Fl.
P.O. Box 7013, Capitol Station
Annex
Albany, NY 12225-0013
(518) 474-8816

In New York State: (Eighth Dept.)
Chief Attorney
Appellate Division, Supreme Court
4th Judicial Dept.
Office of Grievance Committee
1036 Ellicott Square Bldg.
Buffalo, NY 14203
(716) 858-1190

Client Security Fund
Executive Director and Counsel
Lawyer's Fund for Client
Protection
55 Elk St.
Albany, NY 12210
(518) 474-8438

Fee Arbitration
No statewide program, state bar
refers cases to local Fee
Arbitration where available.
New York State Bar
1 Elk St.
Albany, NY 12207
(518) 463-3200

NORTH CAROLINA
Attorney Grievance
State Office:
Counsel
North Carolina State Bar
208 Fayetteville St. Mall
P.O. Box 25908
Raleigh, NC 27611
(919) 838-4620

Client Security Fund
Executive Director
(Address, telephone same as
Attorney Grievance.)

Fee Arbitration
No statewide program, state bar
refers cases to local Fee
Arbitration where available.
(Address, telephone same as
Attorney Grievance.)

NORTH DAKOTA
Attorney Grievance
State Office:
Disciplinary Counsel
Disciplinary Board of the Supreme
Court
of North Dakota
P.O. Box 2297
Bismarck, ND 58502
(701) 224-3348

Client Security Fund
Staff Administrator
State Bar Assn. of North Dakota
P.O. Box 2136
Bismarck, ND 58502
(701) 255-1404

Fee Arbitration
Fee Arbitration Committee
(Address, telephone same as
Client Security Fund.)

OHIO
Attorney Grievance
State Office:
Disciplinary Counsel
Office of Disciplinary Counsel of
the Supreme Court of Ohio
175 S. 3rd St., Ste. 280
Columbus, OH 43215
(614) 461-0256

Summit County:
Executive Director
Akron Bar Assn.
90 S. High St.
Akron, OH 44308
(216) 253-5007

Hamilton County:
Bar Counsel
Cincinnati Bar Assn.
35 E. 7th St., Ste. 800
Cincinnati, OH 45202-2411
(513) 381-8213

Cuyahoga County:
Counsel
Cleveland Bar Assn.
113 St. Clair Ave., N.E., 2nd Fl.
Cleveland, OH 44114-1253
(216) 696-3525

Franklin County:
Bar Counsel
Columbus Bar Assn.
175 S. 3rd St.
Columbus, OH 43215-5193
(614) 225-6053

Montgomery County:
Executive Director
Dayton Bar Assn.
600 One First National Plaza
Dayton, OH 45402-1501
(513) 222-7902

Lucas County:
Executive Director
Toledo Bar Assn.
311 N. Superior St.
Toledo, OH 43604
(419) 242-7032

Client Security Fund
Supreme Court of Ohio
Clients' Security Trust Fund

175 S. 3rd St., Ste. 285
Columbus, OH 43215
(614) 221-0562

Fee Arbitration
No statewide program, state bar
    refers cases to local Fee
    Arbitration where available.
Ohio State Bar Assn.
33 W. 11th Ave.
Columbus, OH 43201-2099
(614) 421-2121

OKLAHOMA
Attorney Grievance
State Office:
General Counsel
Oklahoma Bar Center
1901 N. Lincoln Blvd.
P.O. Box 53036
Oklahoma City, OK 73152
(405) 524-2365

Client Security Fund
Executive Director
(Address, telephone same as
Attorney Grievance.)

Fee Arbitration
No statewide program, state bar
    refers cases to local Fee
    Arbitration where available.
(Address, telephone same as
Attorney Grievance.)

OREGON
Attorney Grievance
State Office:
Disciplinary Counsel
Oregon State Bar
5200 S.W. Meadows Rd.
P.O. Box 1689
Lake Oswego, OR 97035-0889
(503) 620-0222

Client Security Fund
Staff Liason
(Address, telephone same as
Attorney Grievance.)

Fee Arbitration
Fee Arbitration Committee
(Address, telephone same as
Attorney Grievance.)

PENNSYLVANIA
Attorney Grievance
1st District:
Chief Disciplinary Counsel
Disciplinary Board of the Supreme
    Court of Pennsylvania
2100 N. American Bldg.
121 S. Broad St.
Philadelphia, PA 19107
(215) 560-6296

2nd District:
Chief Disciplinary Counsel
Disciplinary Board of the Supreme
    Court of Pennsylvania
1 Montgomery Plaza, Ste. 411
Swede and Airy Sts.
Norristown, PA 19401
(215) 270-1896

3rd District:
Chief Disciplinary Counsel
Disciplinary Board of the Supreme
    Court of Pennsylvania
2 Lemoyne Dr., 2nd Fl.
Lemoyne, PA 17043-1213
(717) 731-7083

4th District:
Chief Disciplinary Counsel
Disciplinary Board of the Supreme
    Court of Pennsylvania
501 Grant St., Ste. 400
Pittsburgh, PA 15219
(412) 565-3173

Client Security Fund
Executive Director
Pennsylvania Client Security Trust
    Fund
1515 Market St., Ste. 1420
Philadelphia, PA 19102
(215) 560-6335

Fee Arbitration
No statewide program, disciplinary
    board refers cases to local Fee
    Arbitration where available.
(Address, same as Attorney
    Grievance.)
(717) 238-6715

PUERTO RICO
Attorney Grievance
Presidente
Comision de Etica Profesional
Colegio de Abogados de Puerto
    Rico
Apartado 1900
San Juan, PR 00902
(809) 721-3358

Secretary
Tribunal Supremo de Puerto Rico
Apartado 2392
San Juan, PR 00903
(809) 723-6033

Solicitor General
Departmento de Justicia
Apartado 192
San Juan, PR 00902
(809) 721-2924

Client Security Fund
None.

Fee Arbitration
None.

RHODE ISLAND

Attorney Grievance
State Office:
Chief Disciplinary Counsel
Disciplinary Board of the Supreme
    Court of Rhode Island
Fogarty Judicial Annex
24 Waybasset St.
Providence, RI 02903
(401) 277-3270

Client Security Fund
Executive Director
Rhode Island Bar Assn.
115 Cedar St.
Providence, RI 02903
(401) 421-5740

Fee Arbitration
Fee Arbitration Committee
(Address, telephone same as
Client Security Fund.)

SOUTH CAROLINA

Attorney Grievance
State Office:
Administrative Assistant
Board of Commissioners on
    Grievances and Discipline
P.O. Box 11330
Columbia, SC 29211
(803) 734-2038

Client Security Fund
Director of Public Services
South Carolina Bar
950 Taylor St.
P.O. Box 608
Columbia, SC 29202
(803) 799-6653

Fee Arbitration
Resolution of Fee Disputes Board
(Address, telephone same as
Client Security Fund.)

SOUTH DAKOTA

Attorney Grievance
State Office:
Investigator
Disciplinary Board of the State Bar
    of South Dakota
222 E. Capitol
Pierre, SD 57501
(605) 224-7554

Client Security Fund
Executive Director
(Address, telephone same as
Attorney Grievance.)

Fee Arbitration
None.

TENNESSEE

Attorney Grievance
State Office:
Chief Disciplinary Counsel
Board of Professional
    Responsibility of the Supreme
    Court of Tennessee
1105 Kermit Dr., Ste. 730
Nashville, TN 37217
(615) 361-7500

Client Security Fund
Tennessee Lawyer's Fund for Client
    Protection
511 Union St., Ste. 1430
Nashville, TN 37219
(615) 741-3096

Fee Arbitration
No statewide program, state bar
    refers cases to local Fee
    Arbitration where available.
(Address, telephone same as
Client Security Fund.)

TEXAS
Attorney Grievance
State Office:
General Counsel
State Bar of Texas
P.O. Box 12487
Capitol Station
Austin, TX 78711
(512) 463-1391

Client Security Fund
General Counsel's Office
(Address same as Attorney
   Grievance)
(512) 475-6202

Fee Arbitration
No statewide program, state bar
   refers cases to local Fee
   Arbitration where available.
(Address, telephone same as
Attorney Grievance.)

UTAH
Attorney Grievance
State Office:
Bar Counsel
Utah State Bar
645 S. 200 East
Salt Lake City, UT 84111-3834
(801) 531-9110

Client Security Fund
Executive Director
(Address same as Attorney Grievance)
(801) 531-9077

Fee Arbitration
Fee Arbitration Committee
(Address, telephone same as
Attorney Grievance.)

VERMONT
Attorney Grievance
State Office:
Office of Bar Counsel
Professional Conduct Board of the
   Supreme Court of Vermont
59 Elm St.
Montpelier, VT 05602
(802) 828-3204

Client Security Fund
Staff Administrator
Vermont Bar Assn.
P.O. Box 100
Montpelier, VT 05601
(802) 223-2020

Fee Arbitration
Arbitration of Fee Complaints
   Committee
(Address, telephone same as
Client Security Fund.)

VIRGINIA
Attorney Grievance
State Office:
Bar Counsel
Virginia State Bar
707 E. Main St., Ste. 1500
Richmond, VA 23219-2803
(804) 775-0500

Client Security Fund
Staff Administrator
(Address same as Attorney Grievance.)
(804) 775-0524

Fee Arbitration
No statewide program, state bar
   refers cases to local Fee Arbitra-
   tion where available.
(Address, telephone same as
Attorney Grievance.)

VIRGIN ISLANDS
Attorney Grievance
Chair
Ethics and Grievance Committee
U.S. Virgin Islands Bar Assn.
P.O. Box 6520
St. Thomas, VI 00801
(809) 774-6490

Client Security Fund
None.

Fee Arbitration
None.

WASHINGTON
Attorney Grievance
State Office:
Chief Disciplinary Counsel
Washington State Bar Assn.
500 Westin Bldg.
2001 6th Ave.
Seattle, WA 98121-2599
(206) 448-0307

Client Security Fund
General Counsel
(Address, telephone same as
Attorney Grievance.)

Fee Arbitration
Fee Arbitration Committee
(Address, telephone same as
Attorney Grievance.)

WEST VIRGINIA
Attorney Grievance
State Office:
Bar Counsel
West Virginia State Bar
State Capitol
2006 Kanawha Blvd., East
Charleston, WV 25311
(304) 348-2456

Client Security Fund
Staff Administrator
(Address, telephone same as
Attorney Grievance.)

Fee Arbitration
None.

WISCONSIN
Attorney Grievance
State Office:
Administrator
Board of Attorneys Professional
    Responsibility
Supreme Court of Wisconsin
Tenney Bldg.
110 E. Main St., Rm. 410
Madison, WI 53703
(608) 267-7274

Client Security Fund
Legal Services Asst.
State Bar of Wisconsin
P.O. Box 7158
Madison, WI 53707
(608) 257-3838

Fee Arbitration
Committee on Resolution of Fee
    Disputes
(Address, telephone same as
Client Security Fund.)

WYOMING
Attorney Grievance
State Office:
Bar Counsel
Wyoming State Bar
P.O. Box 109
Cheyenne, WY 82003-0109
(307) 632-9061

Client Security Fund
Executive Secretary
(Address, telephone same as
Attorney Grievance.)

Fee Arbitration
Committee on Resolution of Fee
  Disputes
(Address, telephone same as
Attorney Grievance.)

STATE INSURANCE REGULATORS

Each state has its own laws and regulation for all types of insurance, including car, homeowner, and health insurance. The officials listed below enforce these laws. Many of these offices can provide you with information to make wise insurance buying decisions. If you have questions or complaints about your insurance company's policies, contact the company before you contact the state insurance regulator. (This list was compiled by the U.S. Office of Consumer Affairs.)

ALABAMA
Insurance Commissioner
135 S. Union St., Ste. 181
Montgomery, AL 38130
(205) 269-3550

ALASKA
Director of Insurance
P.O. Box D
Juneau, AK 99811
(907) 465-2515

ARIZONA
Director of Insurance
3030 N. 3rd St., Ste. 1100
Phoenix, AZ 85012
(602) 255-5400

ARKANSAS
Insurance Commissioner
400 University Tower Bldg.
Little Rock, AR 72204-1699
(501) 686-2900

CALIFORNIA
Commissioner of Insurance
100 Van Ness Ave.
San Francisco, CA 94102
(415) 557-3245
(213) 736-2551 (Los Angeles)

COLORADO
Commissioner of Insurance
303 W. Colfax Ave., Ste. 500
Denver, CO 80204
(303) 866-6400

CONNECTICUT
Insurance Commissioner
P.O. Box 816
Hartford, CT 06142-0816
(203) 297-3800

DELAWARE
Insurance Commissioner
841 Silver Lake Blvd.
Dover, DE 19901
(302) 739-4251

DISTRICT OF COLUMBIA
Acting Superintendent of Insurance
614 H St., N.W.
N. Potomac Bldg., Ste. 516
Washington, DC 20001
(202) 727-7424

FLORIDA
Insurance Commissioner
Plaza Level Eleven - The Capitol
Tallahassee, FL 32399-0300
(904) 488-3440

GEORGIA
Insurance Commissioner
2 Martin L. King, Jr. Dr.
Atlanta, GA 30334
(404) 656-2056

HAWAII
Insurance Commissioner
P.O. Box 3614
Honolulu, HI 96811
(808) 586-2790

IDAHO
Acting Director of Insurance
500 S. 10th St.
Boise, ID 83720
(208) 334-2250

ILLINOIS
Acting Director of Insurance
320 W. Washington St.
Springfield, IL 62767
(217) 782-4515

INDIANA
Commissioner of Insurance
311 W. Washington St., Ste. 300
Indianapolis, IN 46204-2787
(317) 232-2385

IOWA
Insurance Commissioner
Lucas State Office Bldg., 6th Fl.
Des Moines, IA 50319
(515) 281-5705

KANSAS
Commissioner of Insurance
420 S.W. 9th St.
Topeka, KS 66612
(913) 296-7801

KENTUCKY
Insurance Commissioner
229 W. Main St.
P.O. Box 517
Frankfort, KY 40602
(502) 564-3630

LOUISIANA
Acting Commissioner of Insurance
P.O. Box 94214
Baton Rouge, LA 70804-9214
(504) 342-5900

MAINE
Superintendent of Insurance
State House Station 34
Augusta, ME 04333-0034
(207) 582-8707

MARYLAND
Insurance Commissioner
501 St. Paul Pl., 7th Fl. South
Baltimore, MD 21202
(410) 333-2520

MASSACHUSETTS
Acting Commissioner of Insurance
280 Friend St.
Boston, MA 02114
(617) 727-7189

MICHIGAN
Commissioner of Insurance
Insurance Bureau
P.O. Box 30220
Lansing, MI 48909
(517) 373-9273

MINNESOTA
Commissioner of Commerce
133 E. 7th St.
St. Paul, MN 55101
(612) 296-2594

MISSISSIPPI
Commissioner of Insurance
1804 Walter Sillers Bldg.
Jackson, MS 39201
(601) 359-3569

MISSOURI
Director of Insurance
301 W. High St., Rm. 630
P.O. Box 890
Jefferson City, MO 65102
(314) 751-4126

MONTANA
Commission of Insurance
P.O. Box 4009
Helena, MT 59604-4009
(406) 444-2040

NEBRASKA
Director of Insurance
941 O St., Ste. 400
Lincoln, NE 68508
(402) 471-2201

NEVADA
Acting Commissioner of Insurance
1665 Hot Springs Rd.
Capitol Complex 152
Carson City, NV 89710
(702) 887-4270

NEW HAMPSHIRE
Insurance Commissioner
169 Manchester St.
Concord, NH 03301
(603) 271-2261

NEW JERSEY
Commissioner
Department of Insurance
20 W. State St., CN325
Trenton, NJ 08625
(609) 292-5383

NEW MEXICO
Superintendent of Insurance
PERA Bldg., Rm. 428
P.O. Drawer 1269
Santa Fe, NM 87504-1269
(505) 827-4500

NEW YORK
Superintendent of Insurance
160 W. Broadway
New York, NY 10013-3393
(212) 602-0429

NORTH CAROLINA
Commissioner of Insurance
Dobbs Bldg.
P.O. Box 26387
Raleigh, NC 27611
(919) 733-7343

NORTH DAKOTA
Commissioner of Insurance
Capitol Bldg., 5th Fl.
600 E. Boulevard Ave.
Bismarck, ND 58505-0320
(701) 222440

OHIO
Director of Insurance
2100 Stella Ct.
Columbus, OH 43268-0566
(614) 644-2651

OKLAHOMA
Insurance Commissioner
P.O. Box 53408
Oklahoma City, OK 73152
(405) 521-2828

OREGON
Insurance Commissioner
21 Labor and Industries Bldg.
Salem, OR 93710-0785
(503) 378-4271

PENNSYLVANIA
Insurance Commissioner
Strawberry Square, 13th Fl.
Harrisburg, PA 17120
(717) 787-5173

PUERTO RICO
Commissioner of Insurance
Fernadez Juncos Station
P.O. Box 8330
Santurce, PR 00910
(809) 722-8686

RHODE ISLAND
Insurance Commissioner
233 Richmond St.
Providence, RI 02903
(401) 277-2248

SOUTH CAROLINA
Chief Insurance Commissioner
P.O. Box 100105
Columbia, SC 29202-3105
(803) 737-6117

SOUTH DAKOTA
Director of Insurance
Insurance Bldg.
910 E. Sioux Ave.
Pierre, SD 57501-3940
(605) 773-3563

TENNESSEE
Commissioner of Insurance
500 James Robertson Pkwy.
Nashville, TN 37243-0565
(615) 741-2241

TEXAS
State Board of Insurance
P.O. Box 149091
Austin, TX 78714
(512) 483-6501

UTAH
Commission of Insurance
3110 State Office Bldg.
Salt Lake City, UT 84114
(801) 530-6400

VERMONT
Commissioner of Banking and
  Insurance
120 State St.
Montpelier, VT 05620-3101
(802) 828-3301

VIRGINIA
Commission of Insurance
700 Jefferson Bldg.
P.O. Box 1157
Richmond, VA 23209
(804) 786-3741

VIRGIN ISLANDS
Commissioner of Insurance
Kongens Garde 18
St. Thomas, VI 00802
(809) 774-2991

WASHINGTON
Insurance Commissioner
Insurance Bldg., AQ21
Olympia, WA 98504-0321
(206) 753-7301

WEST VIRGINIA
Insurance Commissioner
2019 Washington St., East
Charleston, WV 25308
(304) 348-3394

WISCONSIN
Commissioner of Insurance
P.O. Box 7873
Madison, WI 53707-7873
(608) 266-3583

WYOMING
Commissioner of Insurance
Herschler Bldg.
122 E. 25th St.
Cheyenne, WY 82002-0440
(307) 777-7401

MEDICAL BOARDS

This appendix lists addresses and telephone numbers for state medical examination and licensure boards for all 50 states, the District of Columbia, the Virgin Islands and Puerto Rico.

Data is accurate as of January 1994 and is reprinted from the American Medical Association Library Referral Directory. Because the names and addresses of state agencies may change at any time, you should verify the information by checking in your local telephone book.

ALABAMA
Executive Director
Alabama State Board of Medical
    Examiners
P.O. Box 946
Montgomery, AL 36102-0946
(205) 242-4116

ALASKA
Executive Secretary
Alaska State Medical Board
3601 C. St., Ste. 722
Anchorage, AK 99503
(907) 561-2878

ARIZONA
Executive Director
Arizona Board of Medical
    Examiners
2001 W. Camelback Rd., Ste. 300
Phoenix, AZ 85015
(602) 255-3751

ARKANSAS
Arkansas State Medical Board
2100 River Front Dr., Ste. 200
Little Rock, AR 72202
(501) 324-9410

CALIFORNIA
Executive Director
Medical Board of California
1426 Howe Ave., Ste. 54
Sacramento, CA 95825-3236
(800) 633-2322

COLORADO
Program Administrator
Board of Medical Examiners
1560 Broadway, Ste. 1300
Denver, CO 80202-5140
(303) 894-7690

CONNECTICUT
Section Chief
Connecticut Division of Medical
    Quality Assurance
150 Wasington St.
Hartford, CT 06106
(203) 566-7398

DELAWARE
Administrative Officer
Delaware Board of Medical Practice
P.O. Box 1401
Dover, DE 19903
(302) 736-4522

DISTRICT OF COLUMBIA
Executive Director
District of Columbia Board of
   Medicine
605 G St., Rm. LL202
Washington, DC 20001
(202) 727-9794

FLORIDA
Executive Director
Florida Board of Medical
   Examiners
1940 N. Monroe St., Ste. 110
Tallahassee, FL 32399-0450
(904) 488-0595

GEORGIA
Executive Director
Composite State Board of Medical
   Examiners
166 Pryor St., S.W.
Atlanta, GA 30303
(404) 656-3913

HAWAII
Executive Director
Board of Medical Examiners
P.O. Box 3469
Honolulu, HI 96801
(808) 548-4392

IDAHO
Executive Director
State Board of Medicine
280 N. 8th St., Ste. 202
Boise, ID 83720
(208) 334-2822

ILLINOIS
Director
Department of Professional
   Regulation
320 W. Washington, 3rd Fl.
Springfield, IL 62786

In Chicago:
100 E. Randolph St., Ste. 9-300
Chicago, IL 60601
(312) 814-4500

INDIANA
Executive Director
Indiana Health Professions Services
   Bureau
402 W. Washington St., Rm. 041
Indianapolis, IN 46204
(317) 232-2960

IOWA
Executive Director
Board of Medical Examiners
State Capitol Complex, Ex. Hills
   West
1209 E. Court Ave.
Des Moines, IA 50319-0180
(515) 281-5171

KANSAS
Licensing Supervisor
State Board of Healing Arts
235 S. Topeka Blvd.
Topeka, KS 66603
(913) 296-7413

KENTUCKY
Executive Director
Kentucky Board of Medical
   Licensure
310 Whittington Pkwy., Ste. 1B
Louisville, KY 40222
(502) 429-8046

LOUISIANA
Administrative Services Assistant
Louisiana State Board of Medical
   Examiners
830 Union St., Ste. 100
New Orleans, LA 70112-1499
(504) 524-6763

MAINE
Executive Director
Maine Board of Registration and
 Medicine
2 Bangor St., State House Station,
 Ste. 137
Augusta, ME 04333
(207) 289-3601

MARYLAND
Executive Director
Maryland Board of Physician
 Quality Assurance
4201 Patterson Ave., 3rd Fl.
Baltimore, MD 21215
(410) 764-4777

MASSACHUSETTS
Executive Director
Massachusetts Board of
 Registration and Discipline in
 Medicine
10 West St., 3rd Fl.
Boston, MA 02111
(617) 727-3086

MICHIGAN
Licensing Supervisor
Michigan Board of Medicine,
 Bureau of Health Services
611 W. Ottawa St.
P.O. Box 30018
Lansing MI 48909
(517) 373-0680

MINNESOTA
Executive Director
Board of Medical Examiners
2700 University Ave., West, Ste.106
St. Paul, MN 55114-1080
(612) 642-0538

MISSISSIPPI
Executive Officer
Mississippi State Board of Medical
 Licensure
2688-D Insurance Center Dr.
Jackson, MS 39216
(601) 354-6645

MISSOURI
Executive Secretary
Missouri State Board of
 Registration of the Healing Arts
P.O. Box 4
Jefferson City, MO 65102
(314) 751-0171

MONTANA
Administrative Assistant
Montana State Board of Medical
 Examiners
111 N. Jackson
Helena, MT 59620-0407
(406) 444-4284

NEBRASKA
Associate Director
Nebraska State Board of Medical
 Examiners
301 Centennial Mall S.
P.O. Box 95007
Lincoln, NE 68509-5007
(402) 471-2115

NEVADA
Executive Director
Nevada State Board of Medical
 Examiners
1105 Terminal Way, Ste. 301
Reno, NV 89510
(702) 688-2559

NEW HAMPSHIRE
Executive Secretary
Board of Registration in Medicine
Health and Welfare Bldg.
6 Hazen Dr.
Concord, NH 03301
(603) 271-4503

NEW JERSEY
Executive Secretary
New Jersey Board of Medical
    Examiners
140 E. Front St., 2nd Fl.
Trenton, NJ 08608
(609) 826-7100

NEW MEXICO
Executive Secretary
New Mexico State Board of Medical
    Examiners
491 Old Santa Fe Trail, Rm. 129
P.O. Box 20001
Santa Fe, NM 87504
(505) 827-7317

NEW YORK
Executive Director
State Board for Medicine
State Education Dept., Cultural
    Education Center, Rm. 3023
Empire State Plaza
Albany, NY 12230
(518) 474-3841

NORTH CAROLINA
Executive Secretary
North Carolina Board of Medical
    Examiners
P.O. Box 26808
Raleigh, NC 27611
(919) 828-1212

NORTH DAKOTA
Executive Director
Board of Medical Examiners
418 E. Broadway Ave., Ste. C-10
Bismarck, ND 58501
(701) 223-9485

OHIO
Executive Director
Ohio State Medical Board
77 S. High St., 17th Fl.
Columbus, OH 43266-0315
(614) 466-3934

OKLAHOMA
Administrator
Oklahoma State Board of Medical
    Examiners
P.O. Box 18256
Oklahoma City, OK 73154-8256
(405) 848-6841

OREGON
Executive Secretary
Board of Medical Examiners
1500 1st Ave., Ste. 620
Portland, OR 97201-5826
(503) 229-5770

PENNSYLVANIA
Administrative Assistant
Pennsylvania State Board of
    Medicine
Bureau of Professional and
    Occupational Affairs
P.O. Box 2649
Harrisburg, PA 17105-2649
(717) 787-2381

PUERTO RICO
Executive Director
Puerto Rico Board of Medical
    Examiners
Call Box 13969
Santurce, PR 00908
(809) 723-1617

RHODE ISLAND
Chief Administrative Officer
Rhode Island Board of Licensure
  and Discipline
Department of Health
75 Davis St., Rm. 205
Providence, RI 02908
(401) 277-3855

SOUTH CAROLINA
Executive Director
South Carolina State Board of
  Medical Examiners
101 Executive Center Dr.
Saluda Bldg., Ste. 120
Columbia, SC 29210
(803) 731-1650

SOUTH DAKOTA
Executive Secretaru
South Dakota State Board of
  Medical Examiners
1323 S. Minnesota Ave.
Sioux Falls, SD 57105
(605) 336-1965

TENNESSEE
Regulatory Board Administrator
Tennessee Board of Medical
  Examiners
283 Plus Park Blvd.
Nashville, TN 37219-5407
(615) 367-6231

TEXAS
Executive Director
Texas State Board of Medical
  Examiners
P.O. Box 149134
Austin, TX 78714-9134
(512) 834-7728

UTAH
Director
Utah Division of Occupational and
  Professional Licensing
160 E. 200 South
P.O. Box 45802
Salt Lake City, UT 84110
(801) 530-6628

VERMONT
Executive Director
Vermont State Board of Medical
  Practice
Redstone Bldg.
109 State St.
Montpelier, VT 05609-1106
(802) 828-2673

VIRGINIA
Executive Director
Virginia State Board of Medicine
6606 W. Broad St., 4th Fl.
Richmond, VA 23230-1717
(804) 662-9908

VIRGIN ISLANDS
Administrative Assistant
Virgin Islands Board of Medical
  Examiners
48 Sugar Estate
St. Thomas, VI 00802
(809) 776-8311

WASHINGTON
Executive Secretary
Washington Board of Medical
  Examiners
1300 S. Quince St.
P.O. Box 47866
Olympia, WA 98504
(206) 753-3129

WEST VIRGINIA
Executive Director
West Virginia Board of Medicine
101 Dee Dr., Ste. 104
Charleston, WV 25311
(304) 558-2921

WISCONSIN
Executive Secretary
Wisconsin Medical Examining
   Board
P.O. Box 8935
Madison, WI 53708
(608) 266-2811

WYOMING
Executive Secretary
Wyoming State Board of Medical
   Examiners
2301 Central Ave., Barrett Bldg.
Cheyenne, WY 82002
(307) 777-6463

CONSUMER HOTLINES

The following are some toll-free numbers and consumer hotlines you may find valuable:

AIDS Hotline   (800) 342-2437

Alzheimer's Association Hotline   (800) 621-0379

American Society of Appraisers   (800) 272-8258

Auto Safety Hotline   (800) 424-939

Birth Control Information Hotline   (800) 468-3637

Cancer Information Hotline   (800) 525-3777

Cocaine Hotline   (800) 262-2463

Consumer Credit Counselor Services   (800) 388-CCCS

Consumer Education Research Center   (800) 872-0121

Consumer Product Safety Commission   (800) 6382772

Federal Deposit Insurance Corp. (Truth in Lending)   (800) 424-8400

Free Hospital Care Hotline   (800) 638-0742; (In MD, (800) 492-0359)

Funeral Service Consumer Arbitration Program   (800) 424-1040

Hospice-Link   (800) 331-1620

Investment Hotline   (800) 424-1040

Meat and Poultry Hotline   (800) 345-4372

National Flood Insurance Hotline   (800) 638-6620

Odometer Fraud Hotline   (800) 424-9393

Postal Crime Hotline (Postal Inspection Service)   (800) 654-8896

Second Opinion Hotline for Non-emergency Surgery   (800) 638-6833

U.S. Dept. of Agriculture Fraud, Waste and Abuse Hotline   (800) 424-9121

U.S. Department of Consumer Affairs   (800) 424-5197

U.S. Department of Education, Resources Clearinghouse   (800) 848-4815

GLOSSARY

The following terms are used in this book. Italicized terms in definitions are themselves defined in other glossary entries.

ACCEPTANCE   Agreement to a contract *offer* on the terms presented. An acceptance can be verbal, written or an action, such as the payment of money. Once accepted, a contract is created.

ADJUSTER   The person assigned by an insurance company to determine its obligations under a policy when a claim is made.

ALTERNATIVE DISPUTE RESOLUTION   Also known as ADR, alternative dispute resolution attempts to resolve legal conflicts outside of court through mediation or *arbitration*.

ANSWER   *Defendant's* formal written statement of defense against the *plaintiff's* complaint in a lawsuit. The answer addresses the truth or falsity of the plaintiff's claims and can include a *counterclaim*.

APPEAL   Request that a higher court review the decision of a lower court to correct errors in the application of law or procedure.

ARBITRATION   Method of settling disputes in which the two sides submit arguments to a neutral third party or panel, which makes a decision after both sides present their case. Arbitration can be binding or nonbinding.

AS IS   A sale of a product where there is no *warranty*.

ATTORNEY DISCIPLINE   Act by a state bar grievance committee or court sanctioning a lawyer for violating the state's rules of professional conduct.

BAD FAITH   A form of *tort* whereby an insurance company breaches its contractual obligation to treat its insured in good faith.

BANKRUPTCY   A procedure rescheduling or cancelling a person's debts. Typically, a court seizes all of a person's assets and disburses them among creditors. A small amount, an "exemption," is reserved by the court for the individual—once the individual has been officially discharged of all debts. Under some forms of bankruptcy, the individual must pay back a percentage of those debts afterward, as decided by the court.

BENEFICIARY   The person who is named to receive some benefit or money from a legal document such as a life insurance policy.

BIDS   Competing offers submitted by building contractors setting forth the terms and conditions by which they are willing to perform a building contract.

BREACH OF CONTRACT   Reason for suing based on failure to live up to a legally binding promise.

CLIENT SECURITY TRUST FUND   State bar program in which money collected from attorneys is used to reimburse victims of lawyer theft.

CLOSING   Formal meeting of all those involved in the sale of real estate to exchange documents and money, transfer *title* and finalize the sale.

COMPLAINT   Document that officially initiates a lawsuit. It includes, among other things, a statement of the facts and allegations of the wrong or harm done to the one making the complaint (*plaintiff*) by the other side (*defendant*); a request for help from the court; and an explanation of why the court has the power to comply with that request.

CONDOMINIUM   A form of real property ownership whereby a person owns an individual living space and a proportionate share of the common areas of the housing complex, such as swimming pools and walkways.

CONSIDERATION   Something of value each side gives up in order to make a contract valid. Usually in the form of money-for-goods, this may also be a promise or service.

CONTINGENCY FEE   A fee arrangement with a lawyer whereby he or she receives a percentage of the money actually collected on the client's behalf. If no amount is awarded, no fee must be paid, although the client will be required to pay legal expenses.

CONTRACT   An agreement, that can be oral or written, and is binding and enforceable in a court of law.

COPAYMENT   The insured's obligation to make payments concurrent with payments paid under a policy of insurance. Typically found in a fee-for-service health insurance policy.

COSTS   Out-of-pocket expenses, other than attorney's fees, incurred during a lawsuit or during building contract work.

COUNTERCLAIM   Claim made by a *defendant* in a civil lawsuit that, in effect, sues the *plaintiff*.

CREDIT BUREAU   A company that maintains records of consumers' credit histories for potential creditors who pay a fee for a report.

CREDIT REPORT   A document that shows all or part of a person's credit history.

DAMAGES   Amount of money or other relief requested by the *plaintiff* in a lawsuit.

DECLARATIONS PAGE   A page that summarizes insurance policy benefits and limits of coverage.

DEDUCTIBLE   Monies that must be paid by the insured before his or her insurance company is obliged to pay benefits under the policy.

DEFENDANT   The person or entity sued in a lawsuit.

DEPOSITION   Out-of-court process of taking sworn testimony of a witness. This is usually done by a lawyer from the other side being permitted to attend or participate. The purpose is to disclose relevant information so that each side can evaluate its case before going to trial and decide whether to pursue the claim or settle out of court.

DISBARMENT   Removing a lawyer's license to practice law because of ethical improprieties. This is the most severe form of attorney discipline. In most states a lawyer may reapply for admission to practice five years after being disbarred.

DISCOVERY   Before-trial formal and informal exchange of information between the sides in a lawsuit. Two types of discovery are *depositions* and *interrogatories.*

ESCROW   Money placed in a separate account controlled by a neutral party, to be used in previously agreed-to circumstances, most commonly used in real estate sales transactions. Also known as *closing.*

EXCLUSION   A provision in an insurance policy that explicitly denies coverage for specified losses.

FIDUCIARY   Person in a position of trust and confidence; a person who has a duty to act primarily for the benefit of another.

FORECLOSURE   Taking possession and ownership of real property by a secured creditor when a mortgage is not paid.

GARNISHMENT   Legal proceeding in which a debtor's wages, property, money or credits are taken to satisfy payment of a debt or *judgment.*

GENERAL CONTRACTOR   A building contractor licensed to supervise an entire building project.

GROUP   A collection of people who share a common interest and who join together for the purposes of purchasing insurance at reduced rates.

HMO (HEALTH MAINTENANCE ORGANIZATION)   A form of health insurance covering the insured against most medical expenses for the price of the premium. HMOs control costs by restricting health-care delivery to plan-approved physicians, hospitals and other health-care providers.

HOLDER IN DUE COURSE   In *Lemon Law* enforcement, when financing for the purchase of a new car was arranged by the dealer.

HOURLY FEE   Lawyer's fee based on the amount of time worked on a case. The fee is the hourly rate multiplied by the amount of time worked.

INFORMED CONSENT   A legal rule that compels health-care providers to disclose all pertinent medical information to patients and to receive their consent before rendering treatment.

INFORMED REFUSAL   The right to refuse medical treatment.

INSURED   The person protected under an insurance policy.

INTERROGATORY   A form of *discovery* where written questions are answered in writing under oath.

JUDGMENT   Final decision, announced or written, by a judge deciding the rights and claims of each side in a lawsuit.

JURISDICTION   A court's power to hear and determine a case.

LEGAL MALPRACTICE   *Negligence* by an attorney in the representation of a client that harms the client's rights and interests.

LEMON LAWS   Laws designed to protect purchasers of new cars that don't work properly and which cannot be reasonably repaired.

LIEN   Legal claim to hold or sell property as security for a debt.

MECHANIC'S LIEN   Legal claim by a service person to hold or sell property as security for a debt.

MEDIATION   Informal alternative to suing in which both sides meet with a neutral third party (mediator) to reach a mutually agreeable compromise in a legal dispute.

MORTGAGE   Formal document a home buyer signs, pledging the home as security for a loan.

NEGLIGENCE   Legal doctrine on which a lawsuit is based, whereby the person being sued is accused of failing to do something that would normally be expected.

OFFER   An invitation to enter into a *contract* under the terms presented in the offer.

PLAINTIFF   Person who files a lawsuit against another.

PLEADING   Making a formal written statement of the claims or defenses of each side in a lawsuit.

PMI (PURCHASE MORTGAGE INSURANCE)   Insurance paid for by purchasers of real property to guarantee payment of the *mortgage*. Usually required when less than 20% is paid down toward the purchase price.

POINTS   An up-front fee charged by a lender when granting a mortgage. One point equals one percent of the loan.

PRE-EXISTING CONDITION   A medical condition of an insured that pre-dates a health insurance contract and which the health insurance will not cover for a period of time, or ever.

PUNITIVE DAMAGES   Money awarded to a person who has suffered malicious and willful harm from another person or entity. This money is not related to the actual cost of damages but serves as a punishment and as a deterrent to others acting in a similar manner.

RELEASE   A legal document that relieves someone of an obligation or potential obligation.

RETAINER AGREEMENT   The contract of representation signed between attorney and client.

RETAINER FEE   Money paid to an attorney when he or she is retained as an advance payment for work to be performed.

SECURITY   Property used to secure a debt. If the debt is unpaid, the creditor may take possession of the property in a foreclosure action.

SMALL CLAIMS COURT   Courts which resolve small money disputes quickly and inexpensively. Lawyers are usually not allowed in small claims court.

STATUTE OF FRAUDS   A state law that specifies the types of contracts that must be in writing to be enforceable in court.

STATUTE OF LIMITATIONS   A law that sets a time deadline for filing a lawsuit. This varies from state to state and with the basis of the lawsuit.

SUBPOENA   A court notice to compel the appearance of a witness or submission of documents or other evidence at a hearing; disobedience may be punishable as contempt of court.

SUMMARY JUDGMENT   A court's final decision based on the facts but issued before the end of a full trial.

SUMMONS   A notice delivered by a sheriff or other authorized person informing a *defendant* about a lawsuit.

TITLE   Official representation of ownership that is transferred when a home is sold. Title can be "held" in the name of one or more persons.

TORT   A civil wrong that causes injury to a person or property.

WARRANTY   The legal obligation of a seller toward a buyer to repair or replace defective products. Warranties are express (set forth in writing) or implied by law.

BIBLIOGRAPHY

The following list includes books that deal with various consumer issues covered in this text. Check your public library's catalog for additional materials.

A to Z Buying Guide, by the Better Business Bureau. Henry Holt and Co., 115 W. 18th St., New York, NY 10011. 1990. 377 pages. $14.95.

A detailed summary of the ins and outs of buying products and services, ranging from air cleaners and answering machines to long-distance telephone services to televisions and weight-loss promotions. Also includes mail and telephone order precautions, a directory of local Better Business Bureaus and how to get satisfaction when complaining.

Auto Repair Shams and Scams, by Richard Curtis. Price Stern Sloan, 11150 Olympic Blvd., Ste. 650, Los Angeles, CA 90064. 1994. 195 pages. $9.95.

One of the few books on the market exclusively dedicated to issues of auto repair. *Shams and Scams* teaches you how to choose repair facilities, understand mechanics and protect yourself from rip-offs. Of great value is a nuts-and-bolts guide to auto repair, including information on brakes, the electrical system, smog checks and the tune up.

The Car Book, by Jack Gillis. Harper Collins Publishers, 1000 Keystone Industrial, Scranton, PA 18512. 1994. 159 pages. $11.00.

The seminal guide on buying automobiles. Contains information on what to look for when buying a car, compares specific models on issues of safety, price, equipment and fuel economy and provides tips for arbitration and a "showroom strategy."

The Common Sense Mortgage, by Peter G. Miller. Harper Collins Publishers, 1000 Keystone Industrial, Scranton, PA 18512. 1994. 288 pages. $11.00

Touted as a how-to guide on cutting the cost of home ownership by $100,000 or more, this book discusses different types of mortgages, how the lending system works, how to pick the right mortgage and the types of loans to avoid.

Everyday Contracts: Protecting Your Rights—A Step-by-Step Guide, by George Milko, Kay Ostberg and Theresa Meehan Rudy in Association with HALT. Random House, 201 E. 50th St., New York, NY 10022. 1991. 255 pages. $10.00.

Provides a paragraph-by-paragraph interpretation of the clauses in the most common contracts consumers use, including contracts involving loan agreements, home improvements, car repairs, legal service plans, rental agreements, powers of attorney and assignments. Appendices include a list of consumer protection agencies, Better Business Bureaus and banking resources.

The Family Legal Companion, by Thomas Hauser. Allworth Press, 10 E. 23rd St., New York, NY 10010. 1992. 253 pages. $16.95.

This book addresses issues such as consumer rights, banking, credit, homeowning, lawyers and travel in a question-and-answer format.

The Great American Gripe Book, by Mathew Lesko. Information USA, Inc., P.O. Box E, Kensington, MD 20895. 1990. 374 pages. $9.95.

A readable guide to getting your complaints solved, including information on using free government offices to get your money back, winning a neighborhood dispute and tackling a giant corporation. Also, how to put false advertisers out of business, and how to get stores to refund your money.

How To Buy A House, Condo, or Co-op, by Michael C. Thomsett and the Editors of Consumer Reports Books. Consumers Union, 9180 Le Saint Dr., Fairfield, OH 45014. 1990. 240 pages. $14.95.

Published by the famed consumer protection organization, this book covers the buying process, mortgages, and homeowner's insurance. Also contains information on working with building contractors and how homes are taxed.

How To Get Your Money's Worth in Home and Auto Insurance, by Barbara Taylor. McGraw Hill, 1221 Avenue of the Americas, New York, NY 10020. 1991. 184 pages. $12.95.

Extensive coverage of auto and homeowner's insurance issues, including information about how rates are set, answers to questions for senior citizens and teenagers, and insurance fraud.

If You Want to Sue a Lawyer . . . A Directory of Legal Malpractice Attorneys, by Kay Ostberg and Theresa Meehan Rudy in Association with HALT. Random House, 201 E. 50th St., New York, NY 10022. 1991. 130 pages. $10.00.

This two-part book provides everything you need to know about suing a lawyer for legal malpractice, what it takes to prove a malpractice case and how to assess your chances of succeeding. Lists close to 400 lawyers willing to consider suing other lawyers.

Real Estate: The Legal Side To Buying A House, Condo, or Co-op—A Step-By-Step

Guide, by George Milko in Association with HALT. Random House, 201 E. 50th St., New York, NY 10022. 1991. 165 pages. $8.95.

This step-by-step guide teaches you how to save money by knowing how and when to use—or not to use—lawyers, brokers and other real estate professionals. Includes a detailed checklist for inspecting a house before you buy, a glossary of technical terms and a bibliography of other resources.

Small Claims Court: Making Your Way Through the System—A Step-By-Step Guide, by Theresa Meehan Rudy in Association with HALT. Random House, 201 E. 50th St., New York, NY 10022. 1991. 160 pages. $8.95.

A complete guide to filing a small claims court case, including how to determine whether you have a case, how to serve notice and what to do if you are the one who is sued. Also, collecting the award, filing an appeal and the laws governing small claims court for all 50 states.

Surviving Debt—Counseling Families in Financial Trouble, by the National Consumer Law Center. NCLC, 11 Beacon St., Boston, MA 02108. 257 pages. $15.00.

A must resource for familes in debt. Contents include dealing with debt collectors, fighting back, defenses to save a home and the law of bankruptcy.

Using a Lawyer . . . And What To Do If Things Go Wrong: A Step-By-Step Guide, by Kay Ostberg in Association with HALT. Random House, 201 E. 50th St., New York, NY 10022. 1991. 146 pages. $8.95.

Complete self-help guide to shopping for, managing and working with a lawyer. Also includes fee negotiation strategies, a state-by-state list of grievance committees, and sample fee agreements.

Using the Law Library: A Nonlawyers' Guide, by HALT, 1319 F Street, NW, Suite 300, Washington, DC 20004. 1988. 177 pages. $6.95.

This step-by-step guide teaches you how to save money by knowing how and when to use—or not to use—lawyers, brokers and other real estate professionals. Includes a detailed checklist for inspecting a house before you buy, a glossary of technical terms and a bibliography of other resources.

Winning the Insurance Game—The Complete Consumer's Guide to Saving Money, by

Ralph Nader and Wesley J. Smith. Doubleday Books, 1540 Broadway, New York, NY 10036. 1993. 538 pages. $14.95.

Through guide to personal insurance, including life insurance, health insurance, auto insurance, disability insurance and homeowner's insurance. Also contains valuable information on filing your claim and fighting your own insurance company.

You Don't Always Need a Lawyer, by Craig Kubey. Consumer Reports Books 9180 Le Saint Dr., Fairfield, OH 45014. 1991. 243 pages. $15.95.

A comprehensive overview of alternative dispute resolution and whether and when to hire a lawyer when you are involved in a legal dispute. Includes a list of agencies and industry books offering ADR.

Your Medical Rights, by Charles B. Inlander and Eugene I. Pavalon. Little Brown & Co., 34 Beacon St., Boston, MA 02108. 1990. 402 pages. $14.95.

Charles Inlander, the President of the People's Medical Society, writes a thorough and easy-to-read encyclopedia of patient rights. Information on how to negotiate the health care delivery system and how to report improper care.

Your Rights As a Consumer: Legal Tips for Savvy Purchases of Goods, Services and Credit, by Marc R. Lieberman. Career Press, 180 5th Ave., Hawthorne, NJ 07507. 1994. 104 pages. $8.95.

An informative and quick read on some of the subjects covered in this book. Also covers your rights at an auction.

About the Author

Wesley J. Smith is an author, a consumer advocate and an attorney. He is the author of *You, Your Family & the Law, Legal Rights for Seniors, The Lawyer Book, The Doctor Book,* and *The Senior Citizens' Handbook.* He has coauthored two books with Ralph Nader, *Winning the Insurance Game* and *The Frugal Shopper.* Smith is also a lecturer and media commentator, having appeared before community groups, professional associations and educational gatherings across the nation.

About HALT

HALT — An Organization of Americans for Legal Reform is a national, non-profit, non-partisan public-interest group of more than 75,000 members. It is dedicated to enabling all people to dispose of their legal affairs simply, affordably and equitably. HALT pursues an ambitious program to improve the quality, reduce the cost and increase the accessibility of the civil legal system.

HALT pursues advocacy at the state and federal levels. In particular, HALT supports:

- Reforming "unauthorized practice of law" (UPL) rules that forbid nonlawyers from handling even routine uncontested matters, limit consumers' options and make legal services unaffordable to many.
- Assuring consumer protection against incompetence and fraud by replacing lawyer self-regulation with public control and accountability in systems for disciplining lawyers and judges.
- Developing standardized do-it-yourself forms and simplified procedures for routine legal matters such as wills, uncontested divorces, trusts and simple bankruptcies.
- Creating pro-consumer alternatives to the tort system, such as alternative-compensation systems that guarantee swift and fair compensation for those injured.

To achieve its educational goals, HALT publishes Citizens Legal Manuals like this one and an "Everyday Law Series" of brief legal guides to increase consumers' ability to handle their own legal affairs and help them become better-informed users of legal services. Written in easy-to-understand language, these materials explain basic legal principles and procedures, including step-by-step "how-to" instructions.

HALT's quarterly publication, *The Legal Reformer,* is the only national periodical of legal reform news and analysis. It informs readers about major legal reform developments and what they can do to help.

HALT's activities are funded primarily through member contributions.